CLASSIC MUNSTER FINALS

edited by
Pat Courtney

CAMPUS PUBLISHING

ISBN 1 873223 95 1

ACKNOWLEDGEMENT
The Editor and Publishers wish to express their
gratitude to Independent Newspapers Limited
for permission to reproduce this material.

Typeset by Wendy Commins
Printed in Ireland by Leinster Leader Printing

Published by
Campus Publishing
26 Tirellan Heights
Galway

Contents

The Munster Hurling Final

The Munster Hurling Final ... now there's a mouthful to whet the appetite of anyone who cares a jot about real life.

No ordinary occasion this. It is more of an institution. Steeped in tradition and embellished by the passing of time, it is always something to cherish in the second half of summer.

The mere mention of "the Munster Final" is enough to set the pulse racing, send the heart into overdrive and evoke a host of memories of great games, fierce rivalries and endless controversies. And all recalled as if they were yesterday.

Lovers of hurling will tell you they'd rather see a good Munster Final than any number of All-Ireland deciders. These discerning folk have a passion for the game that ignites in early July and is only sated when the Munster champions are crowned.

Those who care to analyse such things inevitably struggle to find an adequate explanation for the magic, the sheer thrill of the occasion. Truth is, the Munster Final has countless inexplicable qualities that combine to produce an event which is invariably seen as a benchmark for the state of the game.

A good Munster Final will make the year in hurling. Who can remember a bad one?

And while Munster folk themselves innocently believe that they hold "the knowledge" when it comes to their big day, the Munster Final is nowadays an occasion for the entire country to savour.

True lovers of hurling will travel hundreds of miles and further to rub shoulders with their southern brethren. And they will do so again twelve months hence.

Because everyone knows there's nothing quite like the Munster Final.

Victory For Tipp Amid Wild Excitement

TIPPERARY 2-10 : CORK 2-6

The final of the Munster Hurling Championship for 1909 was decided yesterday, and resulted in a win for Tom Semple's team by four points after a memorable contest.

The event attracted an enormous attendance with three bands accompanying the Thurles crowd. The field accommodation was taxed to its utmost capacity, the least computation of the number of spectators being from 8,000 to 10,000. The gate receipts totalled over £150.

Cork Lead at Interval

Cork won the toss, and took the advantage of a slight breeze. Repelling an attack, Tipperary made a dash for the posts, and scored a point within a minute from the start. Cork took up the delivery and sent over. Tipperary continued on the aggressive, and amid much excitement Carew got a chance adjacent to Cork posts, but missed. Cork now got their first point, off a free, and added a second point, after some fine defensive play by the Tipperary goalkeeper. The home posts were again threatened, but the "Tips" cleared to mid-field. Cork returned and Fleming scored a goal, which was followed by a point. Cork was thus placed well ahead.

Play continued fast and furious, a Cork player getting hurt from a stroke of a hurley on the mouth. Desmond cleared in fine style when his posts were threatened. Tom Reardon now scored a point for Cork. Some of the finest play yet witnessed now occurred in front of the Cork goal, and ended in the "Tips" scoring a second point. Cork, however, continued scoring, and added two points, per Hennessy. A great shout of applause went up from the Tipperary supporters when Semple passed to Mockler, who scored a goal. The half-time score was Cork, 1 goal 6 points; Tipperary, 1 goal 2 points.

A Thrilling Finish

On resuming Carew scored a point for Tipperary, who were awarded a fifty yards' puck, taken by Semple, but unavailingly. Even play, in which the Malleton player distinguished himself, was followed by a free to Cork, which led to a desperate struggle in front of the Tipperary goal, which eventually was successfully rushed by the Cork men. The Malleton man and Tom Reardon again shone out in some fine individual play, and both teams sent over. Carew next scored a point for Tipperary, and a centre from Walshe led to a three-minutes struggle in front of the Tipperary goal, but at length the Thurles men succeeded in clearing, and, assuming the aggressive, they ran up two points in rapid succession. Excitement immediately afterwards reached an intense pitch when the turning point of the match occurred.

Semple scored a goal, which gave Tipperary a lead of one point. Five minutes play resulted in another point being scored for Tipperary by Gleeson. Success for the victors of Athy was now assured, and made doubly certain when Carew raised the white flag for Tipperary twice. The long whistle went amid scenes of excitement seldom witnessed. All the Thurles players were chaired off the field.

Tipperary: T. Semple (captain), T. Kerwick, M. O'Brien, J. Mockler, P. Brolan, H. Shelly, A. Carew, J. Mooney, J. O'Brien (goal), W. Smee, J. Bourke, J. McLoughney, T. Dwyer, P. Ryan, J. Fitzgerald, T. Gleeson, F. O'Meara.

Cork (Dungourney): Jim Kelleher (captain), J. Ronayne, J. Desmond, W. Daly, W. Hennessy, T. Mahoney, M. Collins, T. Lynch, P. Leahy, P. Fleming, Jack Kelleher, T. Fleming , M. Shea; Blackrock—M. Dorney, A. Fitzgerald (goal), T. Riordan; Midleton—J. Walshe.

Mr. D. Roughane (Clare) refereed.

Tipperary Take Munster Crown at Dungarvan

TIPPERARY 8-1 : CORK 5-3

Great interest was centred in this match at Dungarvan yesterday, and there was a vast crowd, nine special trains carrying their full complement. The Tipperary Juniors beat Cork by 12 points to 9 points, this match being the first decided.

Great enthusiasm was shown as the teams entered the field for the big match. In the first minute Tipperary landed a goal, amid much cheering. This was followed in another minute by one to Cork. Tipperary scored yet another goal, and Cork again followed suit in a couple of minutes. Thus matters were equalled. Tipperary had the best of the game from this up to half-time, the score then reading in their favour—

4 goals 1 point to 3 goals 1 point.

The second half was pretty even, and a grand exhibition of the manly game was shown, the vast crowd cheering itself hoarse. Tipperary won a hard-fought game on the score given above.

The Dungarvan Band played during the proceedings, and afterwards through the streets.

Clare Beat Cork In Thurles Decider

CLARE 3-2 : CORK 3-1

The Munster finals in Senior and Junior hurling at Thurles yesterday were witnessed by a crowd of nearly 12,000, and great enthusiasm prevailed amongst the large following which the teams had. Clare won both games by a narrow margin. They will meet Queen's Co. on October 18 in the All-Ireland final.

The Senior Contest was very keen. In the outfield play was good, but the shooting was erratic. Cork led at the interval by one point. They fell away in the second half, and Clare, staying the better, worked up a lead, which they retained to the end. Cork made a spurt near the close of the match, which was most exciting. The final score read: Clare, 3-2; Cork, 3-1.

The Junior Final at one time threatened to go altogether in Clare's favour as they led by 5-1 to 1-2 at the interval. Cork pulled themselves well together in the second half, and added four scores—all goals. They were beaten, however, on the score Clare, 6-2; Cork, 5-2.

Exciting Win For Cork In Limerick

CORK 3-5 : LIMERICK 1-6

The final for the Munster Hurling Championship was decided at Limerick yesterday, when Cork won in surprising fashion by 3 goals and 5 points to 1 goal and 6 points. Some 15,000 people thronged the enclosure, which was not large enough for all seeking admission. The railway company refused special trains, but char-a-bancs, motors, and bicycles conveyed big crowds into the city.

Play started at 4.20 p.m. and Limerick made strong running for the opening. The Cork goal was heavily besieged, but Gray was active, and his long pucks relieved more than half a dozen dangerous possibilities. The Limerick team were unfortunate, as no less than seven side-line shots and a few frees in the first half gave them splendid opportunities which, however, failed to realise. Cork displayed all through the better combination and defence.

Limerick, per Gleeson, scored a point in five minutes after the start, and Cork, following with splendid overhead play, did not succeed. Gleeson, from a free, got a second point. Cork then, through sheer good play, goaled, and followed up with a point. Limerick sent wide from a free and Cork from a free, added another point, Lanigan getting one for Limerick shortly after. Barry (Limerick) was replaced by O'Callaghan near the interval, when the score was **Cork 1-3; Limerick, 0-3.**

Limerick's Hard Luck

On resuming the game became even faster, Limerick playing with more vim and contesting every inch of the ground. In a few seconds, they put a goal to their credit in a great scrum. Play became exciting, and Limerick then had hard luck when the ball struck the crossbar. Cork, from a "70" got a point. From a side puck per Kennedy, Cork again got a goal, Limerick following with a point. Limerick pressed and were unlucky in not getting a goal, the ball again striking the post.

For the last five minutes the play was most exciting, Limerick striving determinedly but the Cork combination was too much for the champions, who were defeated by a comfortable margin.

M. Murphy (Cork) and P. Keane (Limerick) were ordered off the field by Mr. W. Walsh (Waterford), who refereed.

Cork: Gray (goal), Sean Murphy, Hassett, Sheehan, Ring, T. Nagle, B. Aherne, O'Keeffe, M. Murphy, J. Murphy, P. O'Halloran, O'Gorman, Lucy, F. Kelleher, Kennedy (capt.).

Limerick: M. Murphy (goal), Rochford, Kennedy, M'Conkey, Keane, W. Hough, W. Lanigan, D. Murphy, J. Humphreys, W. Ryan, W. Feehan, P. Barry, W. M'Grath (capt.), J. Griffin, M'Inerney.

Limerick And Tipperary Finish Level In Outstanding Game

LIMERICK 2-2 : TIPPERARY 2-2

Limerick were first away, T. Mangan sending wide. Working back from the puck out, C. Ryan drove over, but W. Gleeson put on a point for Limerick from a free. Tipperary were held up by Hough, who relieved twice in quick succession, but another hot attack ended in T. Shanahan finding the net for a good goal. The pace was fast and the hurling of a high order. A Limerick advance was stubbornly resisted, and M'Conkey sent over.

In a renewed Limerick attack Power was conspicuous in the Tipperary defence. Limerick forced the play, but the Tipperary backs were unbeatable, and Limerick ground was visited in a fruitless scoring effort. Tipperary were now playing up in dashing style, and the Limerick citadel had a couple of narrow escapes.

A Brace of Goals

A lively exchange in front of the Tipperary sticks ended in an over. Tipperary attacked, but spoiled by fouling, and a Limerick advance found O'Meara sound in the Tipperary goal. Play of a really brilliant order now ruled, and the pace was unusually fast. Limerick engaged in a vigorous onslaught which brought them a brace of goals from Mangan and M'Grath. Limerick's continued attack was well held, and Tipperary went away, but were beaten off by Murnane. Returning, Tipperary sent over.

Hough, who all through played well for Limerick, got in great play amongst the Limerick backs. Limerick pressed, for M'Grath to meet with hard luck in a try for a score. A Tipperary onslaught having been repulsed, Keane sent Limerick attacking, Gleeson aiding well in an attack which ended in an over. Limerick were having something the better of the exchanges when a free brought relief for Tipperary, who improved their position by a point from Hayes. After O'Meara had stayed a hot shot in the Tipperary goal, Willie Ryan, receiving from M'Conkey, notched a minor for

Limerick. Evenly-balanced play of a brilliant order ruled, the fast pace which was set from the start being well maintained. Interval score: **Limerick, 2-2; Tipperary, 1-1.**

Exciting Goal Incident

Play was pretty evenly distributed on the resumption, and under alternate pressure the defences were still remarkably sound. The Tipperary custodian, O'Meara, saved on the goal line, and the Limerick full forward, McConkey, was still engaged in an argument with the umpires when Kennedy put in a goal for Tipperary at the other end. Excitement ran high as the same brilliant standard of play was continued. W. Gleeson (Limerick) and J. Power got knocks, but resumed, and Limerick moved forward. A quick passage close in was cleared by Leahy. A terrific duel followed in front of the Tipperary goal, and ended in an over. Tipperary got away, a vigorous struggle in Limerick ground being rewarded with a "70", which was barely missed by Leahy.

Tipperary kept up the pressure, and Hough covered himself with glory in the Limerick defence. Limerick went away in a flash and forced a "70", which was sent over by Gleeson. Limerick continued on the aggressive but were meeting with a splendid defence. The hurling was now such as has rarely been witnessed in any game. Sweeping down the field, Tipperary sent over. A free from Hough brought Limerick forward, to go wide. Tipperary engaged in a determined onslaught which brought them a "70".

The cheers were deafening as A. Donnelly, cool and collected, for Tipperary, sent in the equalising point with a well judged puck. C. Ryan (Limerick) retired injured, and was replaced by J. Humphreys.

Hough cleared a Tipperary forward move, and Limerick dashed away, but made no impression on the Tipperary backs. Up and down quick as lightning went the ball in play that has never been excelled. This was the order on to the end of one of the greatest hurling games that has ever been played anywhere.

Mr. P. O'Keeffe (Sec., Cork Co. Board) refereed.

Tipperary: J. Leahy (capt.), J. O'Meara (goal), A. Donnelly, P. Spillane, J. Cleary, T. Shanahan, M. Kennedy, S. Hackett, J. Power, P. Power, W. Dwan, J. Hayes, —, J. Darcy, T. Dwan, P. Browne.
Limerick: J. M'Donnell (goal), D. Murnane, W. Hough, D. Lanigan, W. Gleeson, J.J. Guinan, T. M'Grath, G. Howard, R. M'Conkey, C. Ryan, J. Keane, W. Ryan, T. Mangan, P. M'Inerney, M. Mullane.

1922   # Victory for Tipperary Replay
In Exciting Replay

TIPPERARY 4-2 : LIMERICK 1-4

The replay in the Munster Hurling Final (1922) between Tipperary and Limerick, played at Limerick yesterday, resulted in a win for Tipperary by a 7-point margin. It was an exciting game which, on the play, was somewhat behind the drawn battle at Thurles just six weeks before.

The enormous crowd present must have constituted a record for a Munster final. Special trains brought huge contingents from all parts of the Southern province, as well as from Dublin and intermediate stations.

It was a hard-fought contest, for which both sides appeared to have been remarkably well prepared. The hurling throughout was of a high order, though more or less affected at times by over-anxiety. During a thrilling hour there were some exceptionally brilliant passages and if a meed of praise is due to the victors it must be conceded to the van-quished that they gave a display that would do credit to the best hurling combination in Ireland.

For a time the honours were pretty evenly divided, but gradually Tipperary assumed supremacy, and finished up good winners. Limerick put up a spirited fight and strug-gled gamely all the way, and if they were obliged to go under, the greater share of the credit is due to the superb defence put up by Tipperary, whose backs were all the time more than a match for the opposing for-wards. Still, from many view-points, the game was behind the Thurles match. There were frequent stoppages which detracted from the interest in the play, and the result was a foregone conclusion long before the final whistle.

Level play marked the opening passages, Tipperary being first away for Spillane to notch a neat point. After Limerick had bounded away for an over, Tipperary re-turned to the attack and a dashing onslaught ended in Kennedy finding the net for a good goal. Mangan replied with a point for Lim-erick. Tipperary were quick to resume the offensive, Cleary being prominent in a forward drive which was well met by the Limerick backs. The defence prevailed till a free, well taken by Donnelly, brought Tip-perary forward, an over resulting. Leahy for

Tipperary held in a Limerick attack, but the home team returned for a "70", which was sent wide by Gleeson.

O'Meara's puck out was well delivered and Browne sent to Kennedy, who went through for a goal for Tipperary. Limerick engaged in a fruitless scoring effort and returned for Howard to send over. A free for Tipperary brought a goal from Cleary within 16 minutes of the start. Play of a high order ruled till Tipperary forced a "70" which, taken by Donnelly, was beaten off by the Limerick backs, Lanigan just missing for a Limerick score a little later.

Player Sent Off

In a hot encounter at midfield John Power (Tipperary), for striking an opponent (G. Howard), was sent off by the referee. Howard had to be assisted from the field, and was replaced by M. Cross (Claughaun). Donnelly repulsed a Limerick advance, and excitement ran high as Tipperary again moved forward, to meet with a sterling defence.

Limerick worked back to go wide, and a renewed offensive by Limerick was eased by a free in front of the Limerick sticks, the visitors going away and over.

Limerick again pressed, and Lanigan sent wide. A further attack by Limerick ended in an over. Limerick renewed the pressure, but failed to improve their position to the interval, when the scores were: **Tipperary, 3-1; Limerick, 0-1.**

Second Half

On resuming, Tipperary sent wide. Limerick then pressed with vigour, and C. Ryan sent over. Working back, Limerick forced a "70" from which W. Gleeson scored a point. After Hayes had put on a point for Tip-perary, Limerick had an innings for a "70", which was beaten off by Spillane. Limerick kept up the pressure, and were rewarded with a further "70", which brought a point from Gleeson. A Tipperary effort culminated in Power having a shot for goal. Limerick again took up the running and were rewarded with a "70", which, taken by Gleeson, was beaten off by a brilliant Tipperary defence. Spillane (Tipperary) went off injured, and was replaced by Dan Brien (Boherlahan).

Immediately on resuming M'Grath got a goal for Limerick. Tipperary went away in dashing style, and a determined onslaught on the Limerick citadel met with a powerful defence, Hough showing up in his usual capable style. Limerick forwards having missed a good opening, Tipperary returned, to be checked in the goal mouth. Limerick pressed with vigour, and W. Ryan sent over. A. Donnelly (Tipperary) retired injured and was replaced by M. Mockler (Thurles). Tipperary leading a determined attack met with hard luck in striking the sticks. The Limerick backs cleared in capital style, but their forwards finished badly. O'Meara brought off a great save in the Tipperary goal, and Limerick kept up the pressure to go wide.

Hackett (Tipperary) was injured, and W. Ryan (Boherlahan) took his place. Leahy and Mockler put up a magnificent defence for Tipperary, despite which Gleeson worked through for a point for Limerick. Receiving from Hayes, Kennedy got a grand goal for Tipperary. Hurling of a high order ruled as Limerick went away and over. Tipperary had the better of the play, and were good winners at the end.

Mr. P. O'Keeffe (Cork) refereed.

Wild Disorder At Cork— Munster Final Abandoned

Tipperary 1-2 : Cork 0-0
(Match abandoned after 20 minutes)

Only twenty-five minutes' play was possible in the Munster hurling final at Cork, yesterday, the crowd of 27,000 invading the pitch, and the referee declaring the match off.

Tipperary, playing with a strong breeze in their favour, scored 1 goal and 2 pts. against Cork, when the end came with the crowd surging into the goals and over the side-line.

Disgraceful scenes were witnessed in Cork yesterday on the occasion of the finals of the Munster Championships. These were so bad, indeed, that the principal match of the day, that between Cork and Tipperary for the Munster Senior Hurling Championship—this being also the All-Ireland semi-final—had to be officially declared off by the referee.

It was prior to the hurling match that the crowd got out of hand. They tore down the paling at various points, and climbed on to the stands. Appeals by the referee and players were ignored, and there was, apparently, no other alternative but to start the match with the approval of the respective captains. The conditions for play were hopeless, however, and the match was rightly abandoned after 20 minutes.

With the lessons learned from the previous Sunday's Football final at Croke Park, it was the general opinion that some decent sort of order would be maintained. On account of the complaints in the Press, and through other sources, the Cork Co. Board had provided additional exits and turnstiles, but the truth of the matter is that the ground could not accommodate the enormous crowds.

About 27,000 people were present, and long before the junior football match for the Munster Championship was started all the vantage points, side line seats, and stands were packed to overflowing, but when the hurling match commenced the crowd took possession of the playing pitch and despite the efforts of the players and stewards a section of the public continued to crush on to the field of play, with the result that it was long after the advertised time that the players were put in motion.

But still worse scenes were witnessed when the crowd were leaving the playing pitch, and as the majority rushed for the main exit, at the Marina side.

It was a miracle that some serious accident did not occur.

It was a day long to be remembered in Cork, as perhaps never before had there been such an influx of visitors to the city. The teams and some of the supporters had arrived the previous night, and from an early hour in the morning there was a continuous stream of motors and not a few charabancs to be seen entering the city, not counting almost twenty trains, the majority of which were at cheap excursion fares.

The Scoring

Martin Kennedy hit a smart point after 2 minutes' play.

Darcy from far out shot the second point.

Despite stoppages to clear the field, the teams tried hard to give the crowd the best exhibition possible.

A "70" to Tipperary produced another "70", from which Darcy scored a grand goal.

The Tipperary team appeared to have the bigger following, and it is certain that owing to the late arrival of the Tipperary train hundreds of the people were unable to get a glimpse of the play.

The hurling being left undecided with Tipperary leading by 1 goal and 2 points about 5 minutes from the interval, a forecast of the result would be almost impossible, as

Tipperary had the assistance of a strong breeze, while Cork had also the sun in their faces. The attitude and proximity of the crowd, which packed into the goals and reached over the side, undoubtedly had an effect on the match so far as it went.

Tipperary started characteristically with great dash, but the Cork defence were putting up a fine show. Darcy, at centre field for Tipperary, was the star performer, although it took the big Tipperary man some time to regulate his puck to suit the speedy wind.

The match was subsequently re-fixed for Thurles on Sunday next. The winners are due to meet Kilkenny in the All-Ireland Final on Sept. 26th.

1926 Cork and Tipp Draw Replay
In Game Of Shocks and Thrills

CORK 3-4 (13) : TIPPERARY 4-1 (13)

Amidst scenes of wonderful enthusiasm and wild excitement Tipperary and Cork played a draw at Thurles yesterday, in the final of the Munster Hurling Championship. As the winners are due to meet Kilkenny in the All-Ireland final at Croke Park on October 3, the replay, it is understood, will take place next Sunday.

The attendance was roughly 25,000. This would have been improved upon by at least 5,000 were it not that heavy rain fell during the morning and late into the afternoon.

The field had undergone big improvements, the Canon Ryan memorial stand, which was augmented by an open stand, and the entire banking of the enclosure bearing tribute to the efforts of the Munster Council and their local helpers to have everything in readiness for one of the greatest tests in the history of championship hurling.

Long before the scheduled time the stands and side line seats were taxed to their utmost capacity, and the banking was well filled. The rain cleared off and the period of waiting was enlivened by the selections of at least half a dozen bands of which the Cork Volunteer Pipers, who headed the Cork team on to the playing pitch, were most in evidence.

The game was played in good weather, and the rain appeared to have had little effect on the sod. Cork turned out to time, but there was a delay of at least ten minutes in starting, the home side being slow to appear. The players were given an ovation, and the Tipperary captain (Johnny Leahy) bowed acknowledgement.

It was a game of shocks and thrills. Both sides went into their work from the start. The pace was fast, and keen tackling had no adverse effect on what proved to be a ding-dong display of hurling. Early on Cork caught the eye. They were playing with confidence, and despite the prophets, the rainfall in no wise interfered with their stylish and well-combined methods. Tipperary fought with grim determination—vigorous and persistent, but Cork were surely gaining the upper hand on to the interval, when they led by six points.

The score at the interval was 2-3 for Cork to 1-0 for Tipperary.

Deserved to Lead

The feature of the game so far was the excellent defence put up by Cork, while Tipperary, showing no lack of grit and energy, were slow to get into their stride. Cork deserved to lead, but the margin may have flattered.

Tipperary followers were none too hopeful on the restart, and then Cork improved their position. Tipperary now threw their last ounce into the scales, and the game hereabouts baffled description. Resolving itself into a duel between the Tipperary forwards and the Cork backs, the margin was gradually reduced. When Tipperary drew level excitement knew no bounds, and as the retiring champions forged ahead by a goal the odds looked well in their favour.

But Cork were by no means beaten. Time and again they forced the Tipperary lines. Time and again they were beaten off. But in the end persistency had its reward when a well-won goal by Cork once more left the scoring level.

The long whistle sounded soon after. There were feelings of relief all round. The referee consulted the captains, who, it was learned, were opposed to a continuation for extra time, and so, after a hard hour's play, the game remained undecided.

It was truly a great exhibition, worthy of the importance of the occasion and in keeping with the best traditions of Munster hurling. Cork were the more stylish, and perhaps the speedier players, but they did not win. Dash, determination, and dogged perseverance held the balance for Tipperary, and so

the championship is as yet unfinished. The issue is still open.

Changes on Teams

Compared with the team that won the All-Ireland Championship last year there were three changes on the Tipperary side, newcomers being M. Kennedy (goal), S. Kenny and P. Collison. There was one change from last Sunday, Kenny coming on in room of John Joe Hayes, who was later called in as a substitute when Jack D'Arcy was injured.

Cork also made one change on last Sunday's selection, Dr. J. Kearney replacing D. Aherne. This, with the inclusion of J. Kennedy (Carrigtwohill), was the only change on the team that beat Dublin in the final of the National League in May last.

It was of interest to find that the Kilkenny hurlers, who meet the winners in the All-Ireland final, were amongst the spectators.

Tipperary: J. Leahy (capt.), M. Kennedy (goal), J. D'Arcy, F. Hackett, T. Duffy, M. Mockler, J. Power, M. D'Arcy, S. Kenny, P. Cahill, P. Leahy, P. Collison, M. Leahy, P. Dwyer, Martin Kennedy. **Subs:** John Joe Hayes, J. Gleeson.
Cork: Sean Oge Murphy (capt.), J. Coughlan (goal), Maurice Murphy, M. O'Connell, D.B. Murphy, Mick Murphy, J. Regan, K. Coughlan, J. Hurley, W. Higgins, Matty Murphy, P. Aherne, Dr. Joseph Kearney, J. Kennedy, M. Aherne. **Sub:** Phil Sullivan.

Cork Beat

Tipperary In Thrilling Replay

CORK 3-6 : TIPPERARY 2-4

It was, in all respects, a great game, the general run of the play being not far removed from the drawn contest. Skilful in their every movement, and surer in their striking, Cork reproduced their almost perfect form. They hurled with confidence from the start, and did not once waver before the powerful dashing tactics of the opposition. Their forwards could have done better, perhaps, but they were up against a sound defence that drew the plaudits of the crowd in the end.

The veterans, Hackett, O'Donnell, and Johnny Leahy playing well amongst the Tipperary backs, received sterling support from the more youthful Gleeson. Leahy was handicapped with a badly injured wrist, but pluckily discharged his trust during a trying hour. At the other end a quartet of Murphy's, Sean Og, Mick, Maurice, and D.B. persisted in repelling the vigorous onsets of the Tipperary men, but for effective work for Cork in this quarter the palm goes to Regan.

The Cork forwards were fed by Hurley and Higgins, and a trio of Ahernes accounted for the scoring. Hurley was an outstanding figure right through.

Players Sent Off

From about mid-way in the first half Tipperary played a man short, one of their backs (M. Mockler) being sent off by the referee. The Tipperary forwards, of whom Callanan, Kennedy, and Cahill did best, failed to break the tough Cork defence. Out-field there was some inexcusable missing by Tipperary, and hereabouts, too, Cork excelled in speed and accurate hitting. On the whole, the Tipperary side was uneven, and their efforts came in starts and flashes, which were not sustained to finishing point. Mick D'Arcy played well betimes, but was not up to his usual superior standard.

As before, the game was packed with shocks and thrills, and the excited onlookers had many anxious moments. It was approaching full time before the verdict could be regarded as safe for Cork, who led by a goal at the turn over.

There were bouts of really high-grade hurling, but tackling was of the keenest. The pace was terrific, other features being the stylish, but sure, methods of Cork, the dour, determined fighting of Tipperary, and the dash and grit of the two contesting sides.

It was a happy and successful ending to the much talked of Munster final. It was a victory not alone for Cork, but for all concerned, marking, as it does, a big advance in the growing strength and popularity of the national pastimes.

A Huge Attendance

The crowds were larger by thousands than last day, and there was a glorious contrast in the weather conditions. The side line seats, stands, and enclosure were filled fully an hour before the time of starting. The Munster Council and their helpers had the arrangements in capital order, and the stewards, under the charge of that peerless Tipperary hurler of another day, Tom Semple, got through their onerous and unenviable duties efficiently.

Made up of all classes, the huge hosting was honoured by the distinguished presence of his Grace the Archbishop of Cashel, who received an ovation on entering the grounds, and threw in the ball at the start. During the interval the Irish Volunteers' Pipes Band (Cork) played appropriate music.

Team Changes

Cork made two changes, D. Aherne going in as full forward, in room of J. Kennedy and P. O'Sullivan replacing Matty Murphy on the left wing. J. D'Arcy, J. Power and T. Duffy, on the Tipperary side, were replaced by J. Gleeson, A. O'Donnell and J.J. Callanan. The two first-named were injured last day. O'Donnell, who has long county service, was custodian last year when Tipperary won the championship.

Cork, playing towards the town goal, bounded off on the throw-in, but were held up by Gleeson and Tipperary moved forward. In countering the onset the Cork captain (Sean Murphy) was injured, but resumed. Regan sent Cork away and M. Aherne left them attacking. Kennedy in the Tipperary goal saved a rasping shot from E. Coughlan, and the Tipperary captain (J. Leahy) cleared. O'Sullivan (Cork) was injured, but resumed. Cork pressed with vigour, but were beaten off by Gleeson. Good play by Hurley and Regan put Cork on the offensive and the Tipperary backs showed up in splendid style.

D'Arcy sent in to the Tipperary forwards, but the Cork end was crossed without reward. The pace was a cracker and minor accidents were frequent. O'Sullivan (Cork) retired injured and was replaced by Matty Murphy. D'Arcy (Tipperary) was injured, but resumed. After Kearney, E. Coughlan had a good try for a score for Cork, and in a twinkling Cahill sent over for Tipperary.

A spirited assault by Cork found Kennedy saving from Coughlan for the ball to glance off his hurley and into the net for a goal for Cork. After a strong bout of play at midfield Tipperary pressed forward and Callanan receiving from Martin Kennedy levelled up with a goal for Tipperary.

Tipp Take the Lead

Cork went wide following the puck out but again worked back to find the Tipperary defence unbeatable. Fighting every inch of the ground Tipperary got in, and P. Leahy gave his side the lead with a point. Tipperary had gone over before Cork broke through for a point from M. Aherne, and the scoring was again level.

Cork continued to force the play, but M. Aherne sent over. Returning M. Aherne, receiving from Coughlan, again drove wide. Cork returned to the attack, and a centre from Hurley was banged in for a goal by M. Aherne. Kenny cleared for Tipperary, and D'Arcy, eluding three opponents, put over a point from far out on the left wing. Tipperary were again fighting hard for a score when Regan cleared for Cork.

Cork were now leading by 2 points.

A free by O'Donnell eased for Tipperary, but the relief was temporary, D.B. Murphy again putting Cork on the offensive. A hot onslaught by Cork brought no success, and Leahy cleared for Tipperary from a renewed attack. M. Mockler (Tipperary) was sent off by the referee for striking. E. Coughlan, receiving from Mick Murphy, sent over for Cork. D.B. Murphy saved from a lively attack by Tipperary, and Kennedy was twice tested in the Tipperary goal.

Tipperary going forward spoiled by fouling, and following the free Higgins added a point for Cork. Hurley, who was all the time getting in effective service for Cork, left his side attacking. Hackett cleared for Tipperary, and the scene of action changed in a flash. Cahill put the home side attacking, and J. Coughlan (goal) and Sean Murphy saved in turn for Cork.

Weak Finishing

Darcy had hard luck for a score for Tipperary with a fine puck from midfield. Tipperary were again dangerous, and Cahill put over a point from a free. Shortly after Dwyer sent wide for Tipperary, Cork going forward, spoiled by fouling, and Gleeson's free travelled far, but the effort was weakly finished by the Tipperary forwards. Receiving from P. Aherne, E. Coughlan sent over for Cork, and a few minutes later the Tipperary line was again crossed without a score.

In a strenuous tussle Cork moved forward, and were repulsed by J. Leahy, but they returned later for a good point from Hurley. On towards the interval Cork were having something the better of the play, but the Tipperary backs, J. Leahy, Gleeson, Hackett and O'Donnell, were putting up a wonderful defence. At half-time Cork led by a clear goal on the score **Cork, 2-3; Tipperary, 1-3.**

The Second Half

Matty Murphy put Cork attacking on resuming, and J. Leahy cleared for Tipperary. Higgins sent wide for Cork from midfield. J. Leahy again held the fort for Tipperary, and Darcy sent well into Cork territory. Hurley relieved for Cork. Tipperary were working back when Higgins

(Cork) was fouled. The resulting free was saved by the Tipperary backs. A free gave Tipperary an opening, and after a fierce battle in front of the Cork sticks the end was crossed. The pace was still surprisingly fast, and the tackling very keen.

Cork, on the offensive, were repulsed by Gleeson, and in quick time J. Coughlan, in the Cork goal, had saved a stinging shot from Callanan. Fighting doggedly, Tipperary moved in, but a foul marred a likely opening. Gleeson, for Tipperary, saved from the free, and the Cork backs were kept moving in lively order till Hurley cleared.

Hackett (Tipperary) cleared a sharp onset, but from midfield added a great point for Cork. Cork were now leading by 4 points (1-1). Higgins (Cork) retired injured, and was replaced by M. O'Connell. After the Tipperary citadel had a narrow escape, Cork worked back and P. Aherne nipped in a goal.

A Desperate Struggle

The Tipperary backs were again tested but cleared well, and Cahill sent the home side on a scoring mission for Callanan to bang in a goal. Cork were again leading by 4 points (1-1) and they had two wides before D'Arcy opened up for Tipperary.

M. Aherne replied with a point for Cork. Gleeson hit a good free for Tipperary, but the Cork backs were all there. Cork again swept forward, and a sharp attack was broken by J. Leahy. Tipperary went in from a free by Gleeson, but the Cork backs provided a rare stumbling block. Cork again took up the running but went over. A Tipperary onset was repulsed, and J. Leahy was applauded for a brilliant piece of work which ended in his clearing for Tipperary. Cork returned and Hackett saved for Tipperary.

Again Cork worked back and this time were rewarded with a point from E. Cough-lan. Cork were now leading by 5 points (1-2). Tipperary pressed forward with renewed energy, but were held up by Regan and Maurice Murphy. After a tough duel in Cork ground Cahill sent over for Tipperary. D.B. Murphy made an opening for Cork and J. Leahy and O'Donnell aided in a clearance for Tipperary.

From a free beyond midfield D'Arcy's puck brought a "70" to Tipperary. This time D'Arcy lobbed the ball close in, and there were a few lively exchanges before a shot from Cahill was saved on the Cork goal line by Sean Murphy. E. Coughlan (Cork) retired injured and was replaced by P. Delea, and Collison (Tipperary), also for an injury, was substituted by M. Ryan. Cahill left Tipperary on the offensive and Sean Murphy saved for Cork.

Tipperary were still dangerous with Callanan in possession, but Mick Murphy came to the rescue and Regan cleared for Cork. Cork dashed off and Kearney sent over. Hurley again put Cork attacking and the Tipperary end was crossed by Aherne. Cork were good winners at the end.

Mr. D. Lanigan (Limerick) was a strict and impartial referee.

Cork: Sean Oge Murphy (capt.), J. Coughlan (goal), E. O'Connell, E. Coughlan, J. Hurley, Mick Murphy, P. Aherne, M. Aherne, P. O'Sullivan (Blackrock), Dr. J. Kearney (St. Finbarrs), W. Higgins, Maurice Murphy, D. Aherne (Collins), D.B. Murphy (Cloughduv), J. Regan (Kinsale). **Subs:** Matty Murphy, P. Delea (Blackrock), M. O'Connell (St. Finbarrs).
Tipperary: John Leahy (capt.), M. Kennedy (goal), S. Hackett, M. Mockler, J. Gleeson, A. O'Donnell, S. Kenny, M. D'Arcy, P. Collison, P. Cahill, P. Leahy, P. Dwyer, M. Leahy, J.J. Callanan, Martin Kennedy. **Sub:** M. Ryan.

25,000 Crowd Thrilled As Cork and Clare Draw

CORK 2-2 : CLARE 2-2

A crowd of 25,000 was thrilled at Thurles yesterday when Cork (holders) and Clare played a draw as above in the final of the Munster Hurling Championship.

Each side scored one goal and one point in each half.

For weeks past the game had been the topic of conversation in Gaelic circles, and while a close finish was confidently expected, it was never thought that the long whistle would find the figures even. As a result of the draw necessitating a replay, the Munster Council, and probably the Central Council, are confronted with a problem. The replay cannot possibly be fixed for next Sunday. On July 29 the Munster football final between Tipperary (who beat Kerry) and Cork is down for Killarney, and if this is not to be altered there is no vacant Sunday, as the Munster and Leinster winners are due to meet in the All-Ireland Hurling semi-final at Kilkenny on August 5.

A meeting of the Munster Council is to be held during the week to arrange date and venue for the replay, and, meanwhile, the position is in a state of uncertainty.

Memorable Match

As to yesterday's match in Thurles, it was in every way in keeping with the best Munster tradition. From start to finish it was a closely-contested game with the verdict in the balance all the way.

Both sides entered into the conflict with grim determination and not a muscle was relaxed before the end. A level run of scoring added to the excitement, and expectant enthusiasm was the keynote to the end of a hard but keenly and cleanly-fought struggle.

Clare fielded exactly the same side that beat Tipperary in the Munster semi-final three weeks before. The Cork team showed five changes on the side that went under to Dublin in the All-Ireland final of 1927, the newcomers being M. Madden (Redmonds), P. O'Grady (Collins), Dr. J. Kearney, M. O'Connell (St. Finbarrs), and R. Walsh (Sarsfields). Both sides were, perhaps, more hopeful than confident, but it was not encouraging to the Cork supporters to find that their final selection was not decided upon until the last moment.

No Quarter

The hurling, if not all the time brilliant, was vigorous and stubborn, and old enthusiasts were free to admit that the game in general was equal to anything ever witnessed in Munster. Under the non-resident rule Clare had strong assistance from other counties, including B. Considine, M. Falvey (Waterford), J. Gleeson, E. Fahy, T. O'Rourke, T. Burnell, T. Nealon (Garda), J. Clune (Kildare), J. Higgins (Army), and T. Mullane (Limerick).

No quarter was asked for; none given; but withal it was a great game that will go down in the annals of Munster and Irish hurling. A feature was the sterling defence served up by both sides. Level scoring was not an unfitting result and the replay will be awaited with interest.

It was a coincidence that the scoring was one goal and one point each in either half, but Cork were disallowed a goal in the second moiety. Towards the end both sides met with a certain amount of ill-luck and it was a small thing, indeed that would have changed the figures.

The ball was thrown in by His Grace the Most Rev. Dr. Harty, Archbishop of Cashel, who was given a great ovation.

The proceedings were enlivened by the Cork Volunteer Pipers' Band, the C.J. Kickham's Brass and Reed Band (Tipperary), and the Thurles Fife and Drum Band. The field and other arrangements left nothing to be desired.

Cork have been Munster hurling champions since they beat Tipperary in the memorable final of 1926. Clare have not won in Munster since 1914, when they took their first and only All-Ireland title.

Clare: T. Considine (Capt.), B. Considine, J. Duffy (Ennis), G. O'Dea (goal), T. Nealon, J. Doyle, M. O'Rourke (Newmarket-on-Fergus), T. Mullane (Broadford), J. Clune (Quin), M. Falvey (Clarecastle), J. Higgins (Army), J. Gleeson, T. Burnell, T. O'Rourke, E. Fahy (Garda).

Cork: Sean Oge Murphy (capt.), E. O'Connell, J. Hurley, P. Delea, E. Coughlan, M. Aherne, P. Aherne (Blackrock), M. Madden (Redmonds), D.B. Murphy (Eire Og), J. Regan (Kinsale), P. O'Grady (Collins), M. O'Connell, Dr. J. Kearney (St. Finbarrs), R. Walsh (Sarsfields), J. Burke (goal) (Garda).

1928

Cork Win Replay For Three-In-A-Row

Replay

CORK 6-4 : CLARE 2-2

At Thurles yesterday before a crowd that must have numbered close on 30,000, Cork won handsomely from Clare in the replayed final of the Munster Hurling Championship.

Expectations were scarcely realised in the standard of the play. It was a dour determined struggle with the issue keenly knit from the start, and over-anxiety may have tended to extract from the hurling from the spectacular view-point.

There were thrilling bouts betimes, but on the whole the game was disappointing as compared with that of two weeks before, when excitement and expectancy held interest to the end.

There was no lack of preparation by the players, and both sides, if not fully confident, were, to say the least of it, more than hopeful. Clare fielded the same team that had beaten Tipperary, and drawn with Cork. Cork made two changes, T. Barry (Carrigtwohill) and Mr. Leahy (Blackrock), one of the noted Tipperary family of hurlers, coming on in room of R. Walsh (Sarsfields) and Dr. J. Kearny (St. Finbarrs).

Cork's Re-Shuffle

This led to a rearrangement of placings, and Coughlan, who was centre half-back last day, moved to the right wing, the vacancy thus created being filled by Barry. Delea went in as right wing forward, with Leahy in the extreme scoring position, and P. Aherne ("Balty") went back as centre forward. The re-shuffling brought improvement, but it is not stretching things to say that the Cork scoring department is not yet perfect.

The Clare backs did not do as well as before, but if Cork excelled in any particular area it was that their defence, in which Sean Oge Murphy was an outstanding figure, was too good for the Clare forwards. Hurley again proved his worth for Cork at midfield.

At the opening it looked as if the verdict was to be in doubt all the way. Clare were first to score, and after Cork had levelled up and passed out by three points, Clare again went ahead, but were behind at the interval. From this on, though Clare made a few determined rallies, Cork had the upper hand, but it was only in the last ten minutes that Cork decisively proved themselves masters of the situation.

The Clare defence gave way in the closing stages, and Cork romped home good winners.

Brendan Considine, who won the 1914 championship with Clare, and the 1917 championship with Dublin, and is now located in Waterford, pluckily continued on after meeting with an injury to his head in the first half, and showed to advantage right through as centre forward for Clare, but his efforts were not fittingly supported by the front line.

Dublin Next

It is the third year in succession for Cork to win the Munster Championship. Their next outing will be against Dublin (holders) at Kilkenny, on August 26, in the All-Ireland semi-final, the winners to go into the final against Galway, representing Connacht. In 1926 Cork won the All-Ireland Championship, but were beaten in the final last year by Dublin.

The arrangements, as usual, at Thurles left nothing to be desired. When the gates were opened, shortly after noon, the crowd began pouring in, and by the time the big match started at 3.30 every available foot of space appeared to be filled on the stands, enclosure, side-line seats, and outside banking. Everything worked with clocklike regularity: the stewards and other officials got through their duties with efficiency and despatch, and the huge hosting, drawn from all the Munster counties and from Leinster and Connacht, was a model of good order and discipline.

In a curtain-raiser Cork beat Clare in the Minor Hurling Championship by 7-5 to 0-3. Though the score is scarcely representative of the run of the play, Cork were the superior side, but it was a good game, and Clare fought stubbornly to the end.

Play Described

Following a few lively exchanges at midfield, Hurley sent over from a Cork free beyond the halfway line. Cork returned to the attack, and Higgins and Mullane were sound in the Clare defence. The Clare backs were again tested, and Clune brought off a splendid save. Play swung round, and Burke (Cork goal) saved from Fahy. A renewed assault by Clare was broken, and there was a stubborn duel at midfield before Clare

worked back for the opening point by M. O'Rourke. Time gone 5 minutes.

Regan levelled up with a point for Cork. Clare pressed with vigour and the Cork citadel was endangered from a free by Higgins, and later by a "70". The Cork defence prevailed, and Clare ground was visited without reward. From a free about 50 yards out, Hurley gave Cork the lead with a point, and a few minutes later this was improved by a point from Coughlan, also from a free. Cork had then two overs, and the Clare backs were kept moving in lively order.

Scores Levelled

Cork had another free by Hurley, and this was finished by Delea, for their fourth point. Time, 15 minutes. Clare bounded off, and after a free by T. Considine, Fahy flashed in a good goal. The play was fast and keen, but not brilliant, due, perhaps, to close tackling.

The work of the Cork forwards was faulty, but after a lengthy attack the Clare defence was broken for a goal by M. Aherne ("Gah"). Clare led away, and Burke (Cork goal) saved from Duffy. A free eased for Cork, and the Clare backs in saving conceded a "70". Hurley's puck was well placed, and after a few hot exchanges close in M. Aherne got another goal for Cork. Clare dashed off, but failed before a stout Cork defence, and play was at midfield at the interval, when Cork led by 2-4 to 1-2 for Clare.

Second Half

Higgins cleared for Clare at the restart, and later Doyle saved from a free by Coughlan (Cork). Clare pressed forward, but were checked by E. O'Connell, and B. Considine's shot was wide. Burnell again opened up for Clare, but the Cork backs were not to be beaten. Cork had a fruitless scoring effort, and then a Clare move was spoiled by Sean Oge Murphy, who saved at a critical moment. O'Dea was tested in the Clare goal, and the scene of action changed in a twinkling to find the Clare forwards fighting hard for a score. T. Considine, from a "70", had hard luck in a try for a point for Clare.

Sean Oge Murphy (Cork) resumed after an injury, and Cork sprang away, but made no headway against the Clare defence. Clare took up the running in determined fashion, and Regan saved for Cork. Clare worked back, but finished weakly, and Cork led away. The Clare backs were kept busy, and O'Dea (Clare goal) had saved from Delea before Leahy banged in a goal for Cork. Cork were now doing best, but the Clare defence was so far unshaken. Nealon saved twice in quick succession for Clare, and then O'Dea cleared from the goalmouth. Clare fought doggedly away, and T. O'Rourke scored a goal after a tough tussle with the Cork backs.

A Tense Struggle

The Cork defence was again tested, and, quicker than it takes to write it, O'Dea was saving in the Clare goal. The hurling was hereabouts of a high order, both sides giving of their best in a tense struggle. M. O'Connell put Cork moving, but without avail against the Clare backs, and T. O'Rourke opened up for Clare. Sean Oge Murphy came to the rescue for Cork. Gleeson hit a good free for Clare, but Cork worked back, and Higgins and O'Dea (Clare goal) saved in turn before M. Aherne drove wide for Cork. A "70" taken by Higgins for Clare was saved close in, and Cork sprang away for a goal by Delea.

Cork were now leading by 4-4 to 2-2. A hot assault by Clare was broken by Sean Oge Murphy and a centre by M. Aherne was finished for a goal by Delea. Cork were now playing in winning vein, and Leahy took a pass from P. Aherne to score a sixth and last goal for Cork a minute before the end.

Mr P. Walsh (Kilkenny) was a capable referee, but his task was rendered comparatively light by the sportsmanlike behaviour of the players. Mr. W. Hough (Limerick), who refereed last day was objected to by Cork, and though reappointed by the votes of the other Munster counties, declined to act.

Cork: Sean Oge Murphy (capt.), E. O'Connell, J. Hurley, E. Coughlan, M. Aherne, P. Aherne, P. Delea, M. Leahy (Blackrock), M. Madden (Redmonds), J. O'Regan (Kinsale), D.B. Murphy (Eire Oge), T. Barry (Carrigtwohill), M. O'Connell (St. Finbarr's), P. O'Grady (Collins), J. Burke (Garda) (goal).
Clare: T. Considine (capt.), B. Considine, E. Fahy, J. Duffy (Ennis), G. O'Dea (goal), J. Doyle, J. Higgins, A. Nealon, M. O'Rourke, T. O'Rourke (Newmarket-on-Fergus), T. Mullane (Broadford), J. Clune (Quin), M Falvey (Clarecastle), T. Burnell (Tubber), J. Gleeson (Kilishen).

Fighting Waterford Earn Draw Against Cork

WATERFORD 4-0 : CORK 1-9

Ten thousand hurling enthusiasts from all parts of the South assembled at Clonmel, and were well rewarded by two fine hurling displays. Waterford were doubly engaged, meeting Cork in the Munster Senior Hurling final, and Tipperary in the Munster Minor final, and in both the Waterford players surprised all by their keen scientific hurling and grim fighting spirit.

They drew with Cork in the senior event 4-0 to 1-9, and were beaten by only two points, 6-5 to 6-3, by a sterling Tipperary minor team.

Both games were vigorous and keenly contested to the end.

At the start it was apparent Waterford had a strong working combination. They were good at marking, attacking and defence. Three goals came in quick succession per Carroll, White and Butler, Cork notching a point per Donoghue. A stiff battle raged to close the first half, but Cork defended well and secured four more points per Corcoran, Coghlan and Ahearn.

Waterford led at half-time by 3-0 to 0-5.

Resuming on a heavy pitch, Cork put on stiff pressure, but failed to penetrate Waterford's defence. Ware, in goal, though injured, did splendid work. Waterford attacked with dash, and kept Cork defence busy. Keen attack and defence at both ends developed, and the crowd were kept to a high pitch of excitement.

Waterford missed a score, and Cork transferred, and as a result of tense play close in, scored their only goal and added a point soon after.

A "70" to Cork by Coghlan ended in a point, and Hurley, adding another, levelled the scores.

Cork Win Replay

CORK 5-4 : WATERFORD 1-2

The characteristic persistence of Cork was introduced with effect when they beat Waterford by 5-4 to 1-2 in the replay, at Clonmel before a crowd of 15,000.

The game opened in dashing style, and in the first minute "Gatt" Aherne opened the scoring with a point for Cork. Waterford immediately replied, and after fine combination Byrne secured a major for Waterford. When the Cork backs settled down subsequent efforts by Waterford were stoutly repulsed, but in many cases when they missed scores it was in a large measure due to faulty tactics on the part of their forwards. The Waterford backs had their hands full against the nippy forwards of the Cork team. The goalie, J. Ware, showed marvellous skill in some of his saves. After Waterford had a short and fruitless innings, O'Regan cleared for Cork, who held the offensive with persis-

tent effectiveness until three further points had been added to their score per Aherne and Hurley.

Cork were getting a lot of open play, and consequently bombarded the Waterford goal, securing two further majors, per Clancy. Waterford added one point before half-time, when they were led by 3-4 to 1-1.

On the turn over Waterford played with renewed vigour, but Cork were too fast, and beat them at every phase of the game.

The losers displayed dogged tenacity, and went down with colours flying. Grady and Clancy scored a goal each for Cork, and Brown notched a point for Waterford.

Clare Take Scoring Chances To Beat Cork

CLARE 5-2 : CORK 4-1

As a spectacular event the game fell short of that of two weeks before, in which Limerick failed against Cork after a plucky fight. Clare as a team are badly balanced, and the sterling display of their abler hands was in striking contrast to the weaker points.

There were flashes of brilliant hurling, but the play did not run smoothly and the game was remarkable for the matchless defence offered by Clare when Cork tried their hardest to turn the scales in the second half hour.

This, with the opportunism of T. Considine as full forward, may be counted the deciding factor for Clare.

Cork forwards were disappointing and, not forgetting the exceptional opposition, they missed many scoring chances. Aherne had been through a severe illness during the week and did not touch his form as shown against Limerick, but illness also robbed Clare of one of their more prominent forwards, T. Costelloe.

Champions Lack Confidence

Clare were first to score. Throwing themselves into their work with zest and vigour they featured their hurling with dash and determination and seemed to completely upset the Corkmen. On to the interval, when Clare had run up the nice margin of 3-2 to 1-0, the champions had not settled down to their usual style and their play appeared to lack confidence.

Heavy rain fell at the restart and continued well into the second moiety. With two goals Cork reduced the lead and had the closing score of the half but Clare held the lead from start to finish and, all things considered, may be hailed as worthy winners.

Clare last won the Championship in 1914, and it is to be noted that "Fowler" McInerney, who played that year, was never seen to better advantage than as full-back, yesterday.

It is the second reverse sustained by Cork in the Munster Championship since 1926, and the dual honour goes to Clare, who defeated Cork in the opening round in 1930.

Cork are All-Ireland Champions for 1926, 1928, 1929, and 1931. They were beaten in the 1927 final by Dublin. Tipperary, who defeated Clare in the Munster final, won through in 1930.

Goalkeeper's Fine Record

Dr. Daly (goal) won the 1917, 1920, 1924, and 1927 Championships with Dublin, while McInerney and Gleeson also assisted Dublin in 1927. There are others of the Claremen, like Considine, who was an alert full forward, and Doyle with great hurling records. The Army players, Houlihan and Higgins, have been in the limelight with Clare for some years past, and Falvey (University College) was, as usual, an untiring worker at mid-field.

With Clare turning their scoring chances to better account and putting up a great second half defence, the game reminded one of the Munster final of two years ago, when Clare lost to Tipperary.

Clare's Big Following

The crowd, which must have numbered fully 25,000, was larger than that which saw Cork defeat Limerick. Favours were worn in profusion, but to judge by the cheering and rejoicing at the close Clare had the larger following. The arrangements were again in good order and the pitch was perfect, but after the rain a number of the players had difficulty in keeping their feet.

The teams were played on to the ground by the Cork Volunteers Pipers' Band, and prior to the start the National Anthem was rendered by the Cashel brass band. The ball was thrown in by the Most Rev. Dr. Ryan, Bishop of Sale (Australia), who was accompanied by Mr. Sean McCarthy, B.A., President, G.A.A.; Mr. W.P. Clifford, Chairman, Munster Council; and Rev. M. Hamilton, Chairman, Clare Co. Board.

There was a terrific duel at midfield, before McCarthy put Cork attacking. Ryng sent over. Clare led away, and had the opening point by Considine, and soon after Daly saved in the Clare goal. Madden checked a Clare assault, and Murphy sent over for Cork. The pace was fast, and the play keen and vigorous. O'Rourke put Clare on the offensive, and Cork conceded a "70". Houlihan's puck was well placed, but the Cork backs came out on top. In a renewed assault Connery sent wide for Clare, and the Cork backs were kept moving.

Thus far it was a determined struggle, with Clare having something the better of the play. A free by Hurley (Cork) was beaten off, and then Hurley sent over. Doyle effected a timely clearance for Clare, and McInerney ("Fowler") later broke a Cork onset. Clare forwards, receiving from Gleeson, forced a "70" from which Houlihan scored a point. O'Regan sent away for Cork, but Clarke worked back in sweeping fashion. The Cork backs were all there, and when Aherne shortly after forced a "70", Hurley drove wide for Cork.

A Magnificent Free

Aherne, who received from Ryng, sent over for Cork, and in the play that followed the Clare backs were seen at their best. Gleeson hit a magnificent free for Clare, who were rewarded with a "70", and Houlihan's puck went through to the net for a goal. Hereabouts the hurling was of a high order, and Hurley from a free at midfield sent wide for Cork. E. O'Connell (Cork) saved from a lively assault, but a fine free by Houlihan led to a goal by Considine for Clare.

Cork were away on the puck-out, and in a twinkling, after Daly had saved, Aherne flashed in a goal for Cork. Blake put Clare on the aggressive, and after an exciting battle the Cork end was crossed without reward. Clare had their third goal when Considine finished neatly from another great free by Gleeson. Cork forwards were slow to

avail of an opening made by M. O'Connell, and Cork were again wide before Clare moved forward to be checked by E. O'Connell.

With Cork pressing hard for a score, McInerney proved his worth in the defence, and Falvey, at midfield, worked like a Trojan for Clare, who, with speed and dash, were giving the Corkmen little chance of settling down to stylish hurling.

At half-time Clare had the hadsome lead of 3-2 to 1-0.

Cork's Grim Fight

Play was restarted in a heavy shower, and Hurley, from a free at midfield, scored a goal for Cork. Daly saved brilliantly in the Clare goal, and the Clare backs, under hot fire following a Cork "70", showed superb form. Cork fought might and main for a score, but their forwards made no headway against a stout defence, in which McInerney, Houlihan, and Doyle gave a wonderful display. McInerney excelled his best, and the shooting of the Cork forwards was faulty. After a lengthy assault Murphy had a goal for Cork, and Clare were now leading by two points (3-2 to 3-0).

Cork backs held a forward move by Clare, and Hurley cleared at a critical moment. Higgins (Clare) retired injured, and was replaced by T. Mullane. Following a free by Cork there was an exciting battle in front of the Clare sticks, and Daly was injured in a successful effort at saving. A free eased for Clare, and when Cork ground was visited Connery just missed with a rasping shot. Daly was again tested in the Clare goal, but came safely through.

Considine's Great Goal

Clare's backs continued to bear the brunt, but the Cork forwards were outmatched, and there was wild enthusiasm when a clever piece of work amongst the Clare front line ended in Considine getting a great goal. Clare returned to the attack, and a goal by O'Rourke left Clare leading by 5-2 to 3-0.

Daly later saved well in the Clare goal, and McInerney had broken a hot onset before Clancy added a point for Cork. Cork again engaged in a stubborn assault, but the Clare defence was not to be beaten, and there was no weakening by Daly, McInerney, and the others of the Clare backs. T. McInerney (Clare), injured, was replaced by Nealon. With Cork maintaining the pressure, honours were with the Clare backs, but nearing the end, following a free by Hurley, Quirke scored a goal. This closed the scoring.

Mr. W. Gleeson (Limerick) refereed.

Clare: J.J. Doyle (capt.), M. O'Rourke, M. Connery (Newmarket), Dr. T. Daly (goal) (Tulla), T. McInerney (O'Callaghan's Mills), T. Considine, L. Blake (Ennis), P. ("Fowler") McInerney, J. Higgins, T. Burnell, M. Falvey, J. Gleeson, J. Mullane, J. Hogan, J. Houlihan (non-residents). **Subs:** T. Mullane, A. Nealon.

Cork: E. O'Connell (capt.), G. Garrett, J. Hurley, J. Quirke, M. ("Gah") Aherne (Blackrock), J. O'Donovan (goal), J. O'Regan, D.B. Murphy (Eire Og), M. Madden (Redmonds), P. ("Fox") Collins (Glen Rovers), T. Barry, J. Ryng (Carrigtwohill), M. O'Connell (St. Finbarrs), W. Clancy (Mallow), T. McCarthy (University College, Dublin).

Crowd Of 30,000 See Hurling At Its Best

Limerick Beaten By A Side Which Never Gave In

TIPPERARY 6-3 (21) : LIMERICK 4-3 (15)

A wonderful crowd, estimated at 30,000, saw one of the greatest hurling matches of recent years when, at Cork, yesterday, Tipperary won the Munster Hurling Championship, beating the All-Ireland Champions, Limerick, in the final by 6-3 to 4-3.

There was no shadow of doubt about the win of the Tipperary men, for throughout the hour they were the better side. They found themselves in arrears early in the first half, but they showed a wonderful team spirit and fought back in stirring fashion to be on equal terms at the interval.

In the second period the Limerick defence, which had stood up to their gruelling task in heroic fashion in the first half, found the pace of the Tipperary men too much for them, and the Tipperary forwards reaped the fruits that their mid-field and defensive forwards had sown in the first half-hour.

So Limerick, after holding the Munster Championship for the last four years, during which they won two All-Ireland titles, pass out for the time being, leaving behind them a glorious record.

In their place they leave worthy successors in Tipperary to uphold the honour of the Southern Province. The game was a triumph for youth, and the brilliant form of the winners dumb-founded even their own supporters. In Cornally, Lannigan, and Gorman they had a sound defensive trio that held the Limerick front line throughout, while whatever blame could be laid on Butler for the first goal he made full atonement by his brilliant clearances at critical periods in the first half.

J. Ryan the Star Half-Back

Johnnie Ryan was the star of the half-back line, while Maher and Wall, who were marking the Mackey brothers, got through a difficult task with credit. Cooney and Gleeson won the centre field duel against the Ryans of Limerick.

The forwards were a fine combination throughout. They showed great pace, and the earnest manner in which they chased forlorn hopes was proof of their enthusiasm.

Coffey, Treacy, and Doyle roved to great advantage. They were always at hand to help their midfield men, while in attack they showed fine marksmanship. Doyle was the best of the three, and his fine play in conjunction with "Sweeper" Ryan set Carroll and Cross a problem to which they could not find an answer.

Murphy, the full forward, took his scoring chances splendidly, and his two goals in quick succession in the second half sealed Limerick's fate.

Tribute must be paid to W. O'Donnell, who beat his man time and again in the first half to send across accurate centres that only the soundness of the Limerick defence frustrated.

Where Limerick Failed

Limerick were beaten on the wings. Their defence down the centre of the field proved sound enough, but the flanking players were never able to cope with the skill, speed, and artistry of their opponents.

Tom McCarthy, at full-back, has seldom played a better match, while in front of him Clohessy did grand work throughout. Tim Ryan was the better of the midfield pair, while Mick Mackey stood out as the star of the forward division.

The Limerick captain has played many fine games when on a winning side, but yesterday he was magnificent in defeat. Until the last minute he roved around the field, a sore thorn in the side of the Tipperary defence, but he did not get the necessary support from the other forwards, who were completely subdued by the Tipperary defenders.

The first sustained attack was by Tipperary, which T. McCarthy ended with a good clearance. From a free Clohessy put Limerick on the advance, but J. Lannigan was in position and cleared.

Tipperary were hurling with great dash and skill, but their forwards found P. Clohessy and McCarthy difficult to pass. A nice cross by O'Donnell threatened danger, but "Sweeper" Ryan was just too late in his attempt to touch the ball into goal. Keeping up the pressure Tipperary had another chance, but O'Donnell sent wide.

In the next raid, however, Treacy sent to O'Donnell, who opened the scoring with a point.

Limerick was not long in arrears, as a rush down field ended in Mick Mackey beating Butler in the Tipperary goal with a drive from 60 yards. A dazzling run by Mick Mackey spelled trouble for Tipperary, but his centre was cleared by Gorman.

Mick Mackey's Great Point

So far the Limerick defence had done splendidly, and now, after fifteen minutes, their forwards got their chances, but McMahon failed to beat Butler in a rush for the ball. However, a minute later, Mick Mackey got possession well out on the right touch line and sent the ball soaring between the posts for a grand point for Limerick.

Limerick were pressing hard and got their reward when John Mackey seized on a clearance by Cornally to raise the second white flag for Limerick.

A delightful flick by Coffey to J. Ryan was the prelude to a Tipperary attack which ended in Sweeper Ryan beating Scanlon for a goal to leave only a point between the teams.

Just on half time a grand movement along the right ended in Coffey sending the ball across to Sweeper Ryan who had come into the centre, and he made no mistake in raising the white flag to leave the teams on level terms at the interval, when the scores were: **Limerick,1-2; Tipperary, 1-2.**

Tipperary's Supporters Jubilant

Limerick pressed early in the second half, and John Mackey sent in a dangerous shot, but Cornally saved in great style. Then Tipperary broke away downfield, and from a pass by Cooney, Treacy, unmarked, beat Scanlon in the Limerick goal, to set the Tipperary supporters wild with delight.

Tipperary were now on top, and Gleeson led the way to another attack in which Scanlon, after bringing off two fine saves, was lucky to see a drive by "Sweeper" Ryan roll across the goal mouth.

Away came Tipperary again, and Cooney sent the ball to Treacy, who gave to Doyle for the latter to beat Scanlon with a grand ground ball driven from 60 yards.

The All-Ireland champions were now face to face with defeat, and O'Donnell nearly drove another nail in their coffin when he missed a point by inches.

"Sweeper" Ryan had a great chance to put Tipperary further ahead, but he missed his first drive at the ball, and Scanlon stopped his second attempt.

Fighting back in typical fashion, Limerick got much-needed encouragement with a goal from Dave Clohessy. Tipperary, however, were soon back in Limerick territory and Doyle raised their third white flag.

Tipperary were proving too fast for the champions, and it came as no surprise when, after good work by Doyle, Murphy got their fourth goal.

A minute later Murphy scored their fifth, following grand play by Gleeson.

The Match Virtually Over

The match was now won and lost and Tipperary, leading by 5-3 to 2-2, were hurling with a confidence that there was no stopping.

Still the crowd showed no sign of leaving the ground. They were waiting for the champions' usual strong finish—and it came. A free by Mick Mackey started the rally, and Dave Clohessy raised the green flag.

Tipperary proved equal to the occasion, and going back to the attack, a grand cut-in by Wall was finished by "Sweeper" Ryan, who obtained Tipperary's sixth goal.

Limerick went down fighting, as in a closing rally McMahon scored their fourth goal following a pass by Mick Mackey, while Tim Ryan followed with a point, to leave the final scores, Tipperary, 6-3; Limerick, 4-3.

Tipperary: T. Butler (Sarsfields, goal), D. Gorman (Holycross), G. Cornally (Sarsfields), J. Lanigan (do.), J. Ryan (Moycarkey), J. Maher (Sarsfields), W. Wall (Carrick), J. Cooney (U.C.D.), J. Gleeson (Roscrea), J. Coffey (Newport), T. Treacy (Young Irelands, Dublin), T. Doyle (Kickhams), W. O'Donnell (Golden), D. Murphy (Sarsfields), P. Ryan (Moycarkey).

Limerick: P. Scanlon (Galway Commercials, goal), P. Carroll (Effin), T. McCarthy (Fedamore), M. Kennedy (Young Irelands), M. Cross (Claughaun), F. Clohessy (Fedamore), J. Power (Ahane), T. Ryan (do.), M. Ryan (do.), J. Mackey (do.), M. Mackey (do.), J. Roche (Croom), D. Clohessy (Fedamore), P. McMahon (Kildimo), J. McCarthy (U.C.D.)

Referee: D. Ryan (Tralee).

Brilliant Jack Lynch
Inspires Cork

CORK 2-13 (19) : WATERFORD 3-8 (17)

Cork completed the Munster "double" when they defeated Waterford by 2-13 to 3-8 at Cork yesterday in the hurling final.

It was brilliant hurling, with the lead changing hands, and although Waterford led at the interval by 2-5 (11) to 1-6 (9), the All-Ireland champions always had a good grip on the game.

Without Jack Lynch Cork probably would have lost, for not only did he rally the side with brilliant individual play but he also provided great openings, his display in attack and defence being a feature.

Cottrill and Jim Young spiked the Waterford forwards to good effect. Kennefick, Ring and D. Murphy were fast and clever forwards, but the full forward line lacked pace and were up against a solid Waterford defence, where John Keane, Jim Ware (goal), and Hayes were at the top of their form. Barron and Daly (U.C.D.), as well as Hickey (centre-field) were always dangerous, but Chris Moylan was too well looked after by Thornhill, the Cork full back.

In a game in which Waterford missed a few more chances than Cork, victory went to the side with the better finesse, and tradition virtually won the day.

Hoban (W.), Ring (C.), Keane and Moylan (W.) and Brennan (C.) had points in turn before J. Young turned in a grand centre by O'Sullivan for a goal.

Jack Lynch had points for Cork, but a goal by Power brought Cork's lead down. Cork brought up B. Murphy to the attack and switched Jim Young to the half-line. Waterford played in dashing style. Daly had a point and B. Murphy (C.) scored a minor,

and then W. Barron got a goal. A point by Hoban left Waterford leading at half-time by 2-5 to 1-6.

Resuming, Hickey hit a point but Cork surged back to the attack, and from a free taken by Kennefick, Ring tapped through a Cork goal. Points by Young and Lynch gave Cork the lead again, but when a Cork back deflected Hickey's free for a major, Waterford were in front.

Cork hit back after Waterford had missed two chances and points were scored by M. Murphy (2), Ring, and Quirke, Waterford replying with minors by Tobin and Hayes.

Gate receipts at Cork were £1,040, representing an attendance of 15,000.

Cork: J. Mulcahy, W. Murphy, B. Thornhill, A. Lotty, B. Murphy, C. Murphy, C. Cottrill, J. Lynch, P. O'Donovan, M. Kennefick, C. Ring, J. Young, J. Quirke, T. O'Sullivan, M. Brennan.

W. Hayes (Blackrock) replaced A. Lotty (Cork), who went off injured in first half.

Waterford: J. Ware, A. Fleming, C. Curley, P. Dowling, M. Creed, J. Keane, M. Hayes, M. Hickey, J. Doheny, D. Power, C. Moylan, B. Hoban, W. Barron, E. Daly, M. Feeney.

M. Hennessy (Clare) refereed.

M. Mackey Rallies Limerick To Force Draw With Cork

CORK 6-7 (25) : LIMERICK 4-13 (25)

Two goals down after five minutes and still six points in arrears coming to the last quarter, Limerick staged a magnificent rally at Thurles yesterday, took the lead with five minutes to go, and eventually earned a replay with the holders, Cork, in the Munster hurling final.

The game was an individual triumph for M. Mackey, who led the Limerick rally, weaving his way through the Cork defence to obtain himself or make for others the scores that helped his side to share the honours.

He had a brilliant colleague in R. Stokes, while J. Clohessy, the newcomer from St. Patrick's, hurled splendidly in the left corner. Of the centre field pair, P. McCarthy was the better, but Tim Ryan proved a solid partner, and they lasted better than their Cork rivals.

The Limerick defence was taken clean out of its stride by Cork's lightning start, but J. Power was an inspiring force at centre-half throughout and the marking of the backs improved as the game progressed.

What happened the All-Ireland champions was, in racing parlance that they failed to stay and were only rescued from defeat by J. Quirke's goal in the last couple of minutes.

The Blackrock man, who scored three goals, was the inspiration of their attack, with Ring also taking honours.

How the Scores Came

Cork staged a whirlwind start and were two goals up by J. Kelly and J. Quirke inside five minutes. Stout Limerick pressure brought a goal by M. Mackey, but there was no stopping Cork at this stage, and J. Quirke rounded off a hot attack with a goal. Limerick settled down and had points by P. McCarthy, J. Clohessy, and R. Stokes, and Mulcahy brought off some fine saves in the Cork goal before the champions got going again to stretch their lead with points by S. Condon and C. Cottrell. M. Mackey replied with a point for Limerick, but this brought a goal for Cork by Kelly, followed by a point from J. Lynch. Before half-time Stokes had two points off frees for Limerick, and the interval score was: **Cork, 4-3; Limerick, 1-6**.

Resuming, Cork had points from C. Ring and J. Lynch and a goal by Morrison, against Limerick points by Stokes and M. Mackey (2) before Stokes rallied Limerick with a goal from a close in free.

Kelly's point left Cork still two goals ahead coming to the last quarter. Then came a point by McCarthy, and when the mid-field man cut in a ball from the touch-line, J. Mackey sent to the net, after Mulcahy had stopped his brother's effort. Points by Kelly and Stokes followed, and then Clohessy hit a long ball from the touch-line for a goal and the lead.

M. Mackey had a point, but John Quirke restored Cork's lead with a goal, and a point from a free by Stokes left the sides level at the end.

Ring's Wonder Goal Kept Title In Cork

CORK 4-8 (18) : LIMERICK 3-6 (15)

Attendance, 18,000 ; Receipts, £1,476

"The last quarter shall decide"—and the Munster Hurling Final replay lived true to tradition yesterday at Thurles when Cork, after being in arrears from the third to the fifty-seventh minute, crashed in two goals and a point to snatch victory from the jaws of defeat to win their third successive Munster title.

For those who were at Thurles the last-minute goal by Christy Ring, which brought victory to Cork and defeat to Limerick, will remain a cherished memory of a wonderfully artistic effort by a great hurler.

To those who were not there it will be recited for many a year to come how the Glen Rovers' man ran from his own half almost to the Limerick line with the ball bouncing merrily on his hurley and then smacked it across for the goal that won the day.

The Turning Point

Had the referee played the advantage rule Cork's reign as champions was over, for just before their final rally Mick Mackey had walked through to crash the ball into the net, only to find that the whistle had sounded for a Limerick free, which Stokes sent wide.

It was a terrific match, hard, fast hurling, and close scoring, keeping the crowd of 18,000 at a high pitch of excitement, which reached a crescendo in the closing stages when Cork put in their terrific finish.

The new Limerick goalie, Malone, of Fedamore, had a fine game, his saving exciting general admiration. At full back the veteran, M. Kennedy, had a good first half, but, with several of his colleagues, appeared to tire in the closing stages of a hard fought game.

Cooney found Joe Kelly an elusive opponent, but John Quirke, in the Cork right corner, had a quiet game until he flashed into the limelight to get the equalising point in the closing stages.

The midfield duel was keen and interesting. McCarthy and Jack Lynch shone in the open play, but Cottrell was the soundest hurler of the four, for Tim Ryan failed to last the second half.

Outstanding forward on the field was Mick Mackey. Con Murphy tried in vain to watch the Ahane wizard, who bobbed up in the most unexpected places to get or make scores that put his side on the road towards success.

His brother, John, and Clohessy gave the Cork backs plenty to do, while behind them Stokes hurled with his accustomed skill and accuracy.

How the Scores Came

Very Rev. Dr. O'Dwyer, Superior-General to the Maynooth Mission for China, threw in the ball. Limerick had the first attack and Cork the first score, Jack Lynch pointing from a cross by Condon. Stokes equalised off a free, and next McCarthy had a point from a 70".

At the other end Malone saved brilliantly, but before it could be cleared Morrison nipped in for a goal. Back came Limerick, and Mick Mackey sent the ball forward for John to score a goal. Immediately after, Mick Mackey hit a lovely point. After 17 minutes Condon pointed a free to level matters, but then from a grand cut-in by McCarthy, Mick Mackey cracked the ball to the net for a Limerick goal, which he followed with a point.

Lotty retired injured, Con Murphy becoming centre-half and O'Donovan taking the place of D.J. Buckley, who went across to mark Mick Mackey.

Cork finished the stronger, Condon and Jack Lynch, from frees, getting points after

Christy Ring

Mick Mackey, legendary Limerick hurler, photographed at home before the 1980 All-Ireland Final between Limerick and Galway. This was probably one of the last posed photos taken of Mick Mackey at home.

Stokes had raised a white flag for Limerick, and the interval score was **Limerick, 2-4; Cork, 1-4**.

Limerick had a point from a free by Stokes early in the second half, and then, after grand work by M. Mackey, Stokes added a second point. A grand save by Malone from Christy Ring set Limerick supporters shouting, and then Referee Carroll handled a difficult situation in diplomatic fashion.

Malone's Great Work

After 11 minutes Joe Kelly got a goal for Cork, and the issue was in the melting pot. Willie Murphy hit a great free from inside his own half, but Malone saved splendidly.

Then the Limerick goalie earned an ovation for taking down a grand try by Christy Ring from just under the bar, and the third quarter ended at Limerick 2-6, Cork 2-4.

Following a cut-in by McCarthy, J. Clohessy turned the ball in for John Mackey to get a goal. At the other end Quirke pointed, but Limerick were quickly back, and Mick Mackey ran through to get the ball into the net, but was whistled for a free from which Stokes sent wide.

Cork rallied in the closing minutes, a goal by Morrison giving them a chance of victory. Then, from a clearance by Con Murphy, John Quirke flashed over the equalising point, and Christy Ring's glorious effort ended the game.

Shock Result In Munster Hurling Final

Waterford Beat Cork In Memorable Game

WATERFORD 4-7 (19) : CORK 3-9 (18)

Waterford, giving a magnificent display of do-or-die hurling, won the Munster senior title at Thurles yesterday for the first time in ten years when they defeated Cork, Munster champions, by 4-7 to 3-9 in a rip-roaring final which produced a finish as pulsating as any I have seen. The hurling may not have touched classic heights, but the thrills packed into a wonderful last ten minutes will live long in the memory of those who saw the game.

And that winning margin—a solitary point—was a fitting climax to a game free from incident and marked by sporting gestures on both sides. Waterford—the better side well into the second half—found themselves faced with a typical Cork finish but weathered the storm to create one of the surprises of the year.

With more than half of the second period gone Waterford were playing as if they were the title-holders, and into the last quarter they brought a lead of eight points. At that stage every stroke of a Waterford player was cheered to the echo, but a goal from a sixty yards' free by right full-back W. Murphy showed Cork the way.

Out came trainer Jim Barry. Positional changes were made in defence—centre-field and attack. Two more points to Cork left Waterford in danger of defeat; but fittingly enough, it was two of their most outstanding players, V. Baston and J. Keane, who restored their confidence with a point each.

Watches in the Press seats said that lost time was being played at that stage, but the experienced Cork side is never easily beaten and yesterday was no exception.

A defensive blunder by Waterford left M. O'Riordan (right full-forward) with an "open" goal which he promptly and gladly accepted. Only two points separated the sides then, and that lead was reduced to a minimum by a point from Daly.

Ring's Miss

Visions of extra time loomed when C. Ring found an opening forty yards out, but with time to take aim his shot went inches wide of the upright and the game ended with a puck out by J. Ware.

Had Waterford lost it would have been little fault of their own, for after a nervous opening in which they conceded two points in the first three minutes they settled down, produced a standard of hurling which caught the holders on the wrong foot, gained a point lead by the interval, and never slackened until the end.

To deal with their amazing success would take far more space than is available, but I think the foundation was laid primarily at centre-field where J.O'Connor and E. Carew never tired, and it mattered little what combination Cork tried the challengers still remained supreme in that important sector.

It was Carew who scored their first point, and from a side-line shot he placed Galvin in possession for his side's fourth goal.

O'Connor's Big Part

It was O'Connor who gave them the lead for the first time when, with the ball on his hurley, he slipped past the Cork defence to score a brilliant goal in the tenth minute, and it was the U.C.D. man who at all times "shadowed" C. Ring and made it necessary for the potential Cork match-winner to be moved to the attack late in the game.

Yet, without the splendid support of many others the efforts of the midfielders could not have won the game and in this respect goalkeeper J. Ware, centre half-back

V. Baston, and centre half-forward J. Keane, claim the most credit on a well-balanced fifteen.

Indeed, two of the many features of the game were saves by Ware—one from J. Lynch at the expense of a "70" and another a minute later, ten minutes from the end of the first half, from a point-blank shot by C. Murphy. Had he missed either of those, Cork would in all probability have gone into the second period with a lead, but, as it was, Waterford held the advantage at that stage.

Many equally good clearances were made by Baston, especially at the crucial period near the end, and, as a reward, he had the honour of scoring Waterford's last point—direct from a "70".

Invariably the mainspring of the attack, J. Keane was once again the main danger to the Cork defence, and it seemed a strange coincidence that each time the holders seemed likely to go in front Keane added the point which pinned them back again.

Played Their Part

If the players I have already mentioned were the most outstanding, credit, too, goes to A. Fleming, J. Goode and M. Hayes for support in defence and to W. Galvin, C. Moylan and K. O'Connor amongst the forwards. That leaves but few players unnamed but the whole side combined as one in a magnificent victory.

Cork tried every move, but they did not seem to produce movements as good as those when bringing about Limerick's downfall.

The losers' hardest workers were W. Murphy, P. O'Donovan, and their captain and goalkeeper, T. Mulcahy. Considering that four goals and seven points were conceded it may seem strange to pick out defenders, but the weakness at centre-field threw a too-heavy burden on the backs.

Only towards the end did the Cork forwards come to life, and then it was W. Daly, J. Lynch, and M. O'Riordan who moved at speed equal to that of the Waterford men.

How the Scores Came

Briefly, the scoring was as follows: Daly and Ring, points for Cork; Carew, point Waterford; Lynch (Cork), a goal (7 mins.), J. O'Connor replied with a goal for Waterford (10 mins.), Ring (0-1, free), Moylan (Waterford) (1-0) Ring (0-1, free), Curran (W.) (0-1), Ring (0-1, free), Keane (0-1).

Half-time—**Waterford, 2-3; Cork, 1-5.**

Curran opened second half scoring with a goal for Waterford (2 mins.), Daly (Cork) and Keane exchanged points; Galvin goal for Waterford, Carew (0-1); W. Murphy (Cork), goal from free; C. Murphy (0-1), J. Lynch (0-1), Keane then added a point for Waterford and Baston a second.

A goal in lost time for Cork was scored by O'Riordan, and in the closing minutes Daly reduced the lead to a single point.

Waterford: J. Wall; A Fleming, J. Cusack, J. Goode; D. Power, V. Baston, M. Hayes; J. O'Connor, D. Carew; W. Galvin, J. Keane, C. Moylan; K. O'Connor, F. Daly, T. Curran. **Sub:** L. Fanning replaced Power (injured).

Cork: T. Mulcahy; W. Murphy, C. Murphy, M. Tuohy; J. West, P. O'Donovan, J. Young; C. Ring, B. Murphy; J. Hartnett, W. Daly, C. Murphy; M. O'Riordan, E.J. O'Sullivan, J. Lynch. **Sub:** J. Twomey replaced West (injured).

Referee: Mr. J. Roche (Limerick).

Cork Easily Mastered Tipperary Challenge

CORK 3-10 : TIPPERARY 1-11

Tipperary folk may with no little justice rail the elements that the hay is not yet saved, but they can have no growl whatever that Cork are not "bet", as in the Munster Senior Hurling championship final at the Gaelic Grounds, Limerick, yesterday, the All-Ireland title-holders were much more the superior side than the final tally of 3-10 to 1-11 would lead one to believe.

A record crowd of 46,265 came in anticipation of seeing the Munster decider to eclipse them all, ignoring the very menacing conditions—there were torrential forenoon showers—but I have no hesitation in saying that I have witnessed and enjoyed many incomparably better southern finals.

For one thing, at an early stage the encounter lacked a game's greatest of all attractions—uncertainty as to the outcome—and at half-time, when Tipperary led by but a paltry four points after having had the backing of a considerable wind, there was little doubt about the final destination of honours.

On top of that there were some quite undistinguished passages of hurling and what might most appropriately be described as much rank poor striking by the Tipperary men.

Those points are not made in disparagement of Cork's achievement, and but for some wondrous saves by Reddan they would have had a margin more illustrative of their over-all dominance—but a year from now I venture to suggest that the only vivid recollection of the hour will be the almost incredible artistry of the greatest hurler of them all, the one and only Christy Ring.

Lacked Tension

The game was far from being dissatisfying, but it did lack the quite legitimate fire and tension of the first half of the Kilkenny-Wexford Leinster final of a week earlier.

Yet, despite the comparative shortcomings of the hour, the winners would be quite warranted in hailing their performance.

Yesterday they were a better side than that which won out last year, and at this stage—although much water will flow under the bridge between now and September—I would rate them favourites of the trio now remaining in the race for highest honours.

Even though the Tipperary attack lacked very essential "devil", there was no doubting the accomplished competence of the Cork rearguard, in which D. Hayes, new to the centre half berth, blotted out a succession of Tipperary 40 yards men.

The Blackrock's man's arrival in such assured fashion adds much to the solidity of the half line, and surely at this stage of their careers one does not need to say that the last line is as good as there is, or has been, in the game for a long time.

The midfield remains the problem of the side, but on the lesson of yesterday's hour a forward line which includes Ring is quite capable of combating such an unfavourable condition of things.

What of Tipperary? Well, if I am not mistaken, we saw unmistakeable signs that the greatest days of what might loosely be termed the 1949-51 side are over, and that Tommy Doyle, that great ornament of the game since 1937, is at last feeling the toll of the years.

Same Old Story

As far as the losers' forwards were concerned it was just the story of the League decider in different setting. The statistician might point out that they were no more culpable than Cork's, inasmuch as their total of thirteen wides was only two greater than the winners.

But there was utterly no comparison between the two units. Every time Cork had the ball within what one might term range, a score looked imminent, while I always had the impression that a Tipperary goal was a very remote possibility.

It was that feeling in the end proved well founded, that in a sense denuded the game.

Bannon tried with all the virility and skill associated with his game, but as far as effect was concerned the support of his efforts was little more than of the token variety.

The losers' defence, too, lost something of its rating. Finn was the star of that department, completely shutting out Hartnett, and the effect of his superintending rather than "policing" of the centre-forward was seen when the coming on of Coffey caused a re-shuffle which brought J. Doyle to centre-half.

Stakelum and Hough had moments of majesty at mid-field, but their work was not nearly consistent enough to compensate for the shortcomings of the men up in front.

That Man Again

But to get back to Cork, one must ask what manner of man is this Ring? Yearly he becomes even more a prodigy and I have not the slightest doubt that Tipperary would have won as readily as Cork had he been wearing a blue and gold jersey.

He may have had his quiet moments yesterday, being beaten now and again, but the superlative quality of what he achieved must, now that the "pill" has been swallowed, be enjoyable in retrospect to Tipperary men.

One could exhaust a store of adjectives and yet fail to distinguish the Glen Rovers' wizard adequately from his fellows, teammates and opponents.

Barry's Fine Game

Next to him in the attack I place Barry who repaid with compound interest some joyous hours that Byrne has had at his expense. Dowling also was ever a menace to the Tipperary posts, and Hartnett celebrated his parole when Finn was transferred to mark Ring.

Every man in Cork's defence has reason to remember the hour with the utmost satisfaction and, as I have already said, all I feel disposed to say about the midfield, that about closes the case, other than to mention that the champions are now in the All-Ireland final.

How Scores Came

Cork were the first to make any appreciable ground and when T. Doyle conceded a free Ring shot hard and low.

The ball hopped before reaching the square and seemed to be going wide but went in off a Tipperary defender's boot for a goal within half a minute of the start.

Tipperary were placed on the offensive by Reddan's goal puck, but the forward shot the first of a series of wides before Shanahan opened the challengers' account with a point from a free.

Three minutes later Ring negatived from another placed ball and near the end of the quarter Murphy put the champions further ahead with a great point from midfield.

Tipperary now reshuffled their attack and in the sixteenth minute Shanahan pointed another free. That score was the signal for a succession of Tipperary flags as a minute later the same player had a point from play. In less time that it takes to tell, Shanahan had another point from a free and then after a 21 yards free by Kenny had been stopped but not cleared, Stakelum was on the spot to gather and shoot a goal.

Bannon (2) and Shanahan had further points before Hartnett answered with a like score for Cork. Before the interval Shanahan and Ring each had points from frees.

Half-time Tipperary, 1-8; Cork, 1-4.

Champions Hit Back

Three minutes after the restart, Stakelum put Tipperary further ahead with a point, but instantly Ring answered with a like score for Cork.

The champions maintained the offensive, and when Reddan saved a bullet-like shot from Hartnett, Dowling was on the spot to goal. A minute later Ring fastened on an exceedingly rash clearance by a Tipperary defender and leisurely picked up to score a point, the equaliser.

The winners were now rampant, and,

Dapper Jim Barry, trainer of the successful Cork team

following a hectic mill in the Tipperary goal area, Kelly goaled, to establish a lead that Cork never surrendered.

Shortly afterwards Shanahan kept the losers in the hunt with a point from a free far out on the wing and then we had six minutes during which Tipperary had the edge, but failed to add to their tally.

Just at the end of the third quarter Ring put his side further ahead with a point. Five minutes later he had a similar score from a free, and before the end he had two more points with efforts that were typical of the man. In the first minute of lost time Shanahan had the last score of the match, a point for the losers.

Tipperary: A. Reddan, M. Byrne, A. Brennan, J. Doyle, C. Keane, J. Finn, T. Doyle (capt.), P. Stakelum, J. Hough, N. Ryan, P. Shanahan, S. Bannon, T. Ryan, P. Kenny, P. Maher. **Subs:** G. Doyle (for T. Ryan), F. Coffey (for Keane), Tommy Ryan (for P. Maher).

Cork: D Creedon, G. O'Riordan, J. Lyons, A. O'Shaughnessy, M. Fouhy, D. Hayes, V. Twomey, J. Twomey, G. Murphy, W.J. Daly, J. Hartnett, C. Ring (capt.), T. Kelly, L. Dowling, P. Barry. **Sub:** J. Lynam (for J. Twomey).

Referee: W. O'Donoghue (Limerick).

Crushing Defeat for Munster Holders

Waterford's Early Fade-out As Tipperary Romp To Title Triumph

TIPPERARY 4-12 : WATERFORD 1-5

The Munster senior hurling champions, Waterford, were demolished 4-12 to 1-5 at Thurles Sportsfield yesterday by a Tipperary team that hurled with devastating but quite legitimate fury, in a southern decider that was as good as over just after the second quarter, when the challengers led by 2-5 to 1-2. The lead was by no means an intimidating one, but even at that stage there was a disparity between the teams throughout the field that made the result inevitable.

At the interval, Tipperary led by 3-8 to 1-2, and although Waterford made a game effort after the restart, their endeavours were futile against the winners' defence which performed even better than against Cork—and that is praise indeed.

Silenced

The game, played in pleasant but overcast conditions, attracted an attendance of 31,384, but after twenty minutes they were the most mute Munster final gathering I have ever known.

In the exultation of victory Tipperary folk were hailing their forward line of the newly-discovered power, but celebration of the end of the barren period—it began in 1952—over, I feel that supporters, while reassured beyond measure about the future, will refuse to believe that their attack is as good as it looked yesterday, when it seemed a superlative set-up.

Waterford, as I saw them, were a team without a midfield, opposed by a side which had one of the very best half-back lines I have ever seen, while Tipperary's midfielders, Theo English and John Hough, who seemed to rejoice in his return to the team, hurled so well that one often wondered where were their opposite numbers.

But even had the losers claimed parity in that vital area, I wonder if it would have availed them anything, such was the sheer brilliance of the Tipperary half-back line of Jimmy Finn, Tony Wall and John Doyle.

All three were positively magnificent, and it is no reflection on the prowess of Finn and Wall to say that they were overshadowed by Doyle—the hardihood of the man is astonishing.

Tireless Efforts

With an assurance that savoured of contempt, he hurled Mick Flannelly and Larry Guinan in turn into the ground and, as if seeking new worlds to conquer, he tore into other rivals as eagerly as if he had been starved of hurling for weeks, if not months.

Not unnaturally, he took a lot of punishment in a contest in which every man comported himself in exemplary manner, but each succeeding weal seemed but to strengthen his resolve to make all his other great games for Tipperary seem but trifling contributions.

True enough, the Waterford half-back line was not great, but such was the ineptitude of the losers' midfield and half-line of attack that the full-back line can wash their hands unsullied of the defeat.

Best of the first line of defence was Mick Lacey who did very well, although pitted against Donie Nealon.

Easiest Ever

Such was Tipperary's difficult passage—they also had to dispose of Limerick and Cork—that followers will not forget this return to eminence, but I wonder if the county has ever had a more facile victory in a southern final.

In the first ten minutes, during which it

seemed that the speed of the Waterford men might prove a rare problem for the opposition, the losers' mid-field was always struggling, but had not yet been "found out", and once it was, the possibility of the 1958 Munster decider proving an epic encounter had evaporated in the heavy atmosphere.

Having seen just cause to "slate" the Tipperary attack, afrer the poverty of their hurling against Cork, it is but meet that they should be hailed on their performance of yesterday.

John Doyle: "With an assurance that savoured of contempt, he hurled Mick Flannelly and Larry Guinan in turn into the ground and, as if seeking new worlds to conquer, he tore into other rivals as eagerly as if he had been starved of hurling for weeks, if not months."

It seemed hard to believe that these were the six forwards that played against Cork. But the same men they were; and of the sextet I was most taken by the improvement in the form of Larry Keane who truly lived up to his Thurles rating.

Again Impressive

Donie Nealon was again so good, so zestful and so daring that I feel the U.C.D. man is sure to become a great figure of the game.

Liam Connolly, too, had a great hour and is without doubt the best corner forward Tipperary have had since the great Paddy Kenny's star began to set.

Jimmy Doyle is obviously capable of more than he has yet achieved, but full-forward John McGrath has yet to prove himself worthy of inclusion; and Tom Larkin would be much more effective if he did not try to do too much every time.

One must also refer to the herculean work of the winners' full-back, Mick Maher, who was superlative, and Kieran Carey. The years, however, seem to be catching up on Micky Byrne.

No Answer

What of Waterford? One is not unmindful of how they battled so gamely in a forlorn cause, but they had no answer to the power hurling of the winners' defence and midfield and, despite the valour of the work of Austin Flynn and Lacey, their defence was quite unequal to the task of holding a transformed Tipperary forward division.

Even the great work of that pair would not have saved the title-holders from a rout had not Ned Power in goal proved himself a man of eagle eye and lion-hearted courage.

It illustrated the distress of Waterford that in the second half, which they most injudiciously started with Phil Grimes and Seamus Power still at midfield, the switches in attack were almost bewildering.

The Scoring

Fifty seconds after the throw-in Tipperary took the lead when McGrath diverted an English centre to the Waterford net. Within half a minute Kiely had a beauty of a point for Waterford, and then, following a weak goal puck by John O'Grady, Mick Flannelly goaled with a shot that O'Grady who later did very well, should have saved.

Tipperary then had points by Wall from a "70", Keane, Nealon, Connolly and Jimmy Doyle. Waterford replied with a point by Phil Grimes, after what seemed a certain point had been signalled wide by an umpire.

Tipperary quickly regained the mastery, and Connolly and Keane put on great Tipperary goals, for which English and Jimmy Doyle could claim much of the credit. Young Doyle followed with a great point and before the interval Nealon (free) and Hough increased Tipperary's lead with points.

Half-time: Tipperary, 3-8; Waterford, 1-2.

Two minutes after the restart Waterford had a point from a 75 yards free by Lacey. Tipperary answered with a superb point by Nealon in the eighth minute, and just at the start of the last quarter Seamus Power sent over the bar for Waterford.

Hopes of a revival by the title holders were killed two minutes later, when Connolly proved his worth in snatching a great goal. John Kiely, on the "40" for some time, had a point for Waterford, but Tipperary quickly regained the upper hand and had three points by Jimmy Doyle, two of them wonderful efforts from play and the other from a free.

Tailpiece: Moss Walsh (Cork) handled the game so well that I feel that the demand on his services will be many in the future. How I sighed for a Tom Semple, as good a steward as he was a hurler, as in the closing stages spectators trekked down the sideline, obscuring the view of those whose homes did not appear to be on fire.

Tipperary: J. O'Grady; M. Byrne, M. Maher, K. Carey; J. Finn, T. Wall (capt.), John Doyle; T. English, J. Hough; D. Nealon, T. Larkin, Jimmy Doyle; L. Keane, J. McGrath, L. Connolly.

Waterford: N. Power; T. Cunningham, A. Flynn, J. Barron; J. Condon, M. Og. Morrissey, M. Lacey; P. Grimes, S. Power (capt.); M. Flannelly, T. Cheasty, F. Walsh; L. Guinan, J. Kiely, D. Whelan. **Subs:** J. Harney (for Condon), W. Dunphy (for Whelan).

Referee: M. Walsh (Cork).

Tipperary Survive To Win At Thurles

TIPPERARY 4-13 : CORK 4-11

Although the passage of time hallows memories and causes us to add colour to great games of the past, many will state without reserve that never have they seen such a fierce combat as the Munster senior hurling final in which Tipperary defeated Cork by 4-13 to 4-11 at Thurles Sportsfield yesterday before an attendance of 49,670.

This was a game that made one marvel at the hardihood of the human frame, as every man pursued the ball with a zeal that was breathtaking in its intensity and resolution.

Indeed, never have I seen men on a hurling field who were so utterly contemptuous of their personal safety when duty called.

Having seen every Munster final since 1922, I feel entitled to tie a tag on this match; and it is with the utmost confidence that I assert that this Thurles game must have been as furious a Munster decider as was ever played.

The fare was not in the classical mould, but there was no room for ornate work in a hurling frenzy, the atmosphere of which was at times almost alarming.

Although torrential rain had drenched many to the skin during the minor match, not a person in the ground left before the end of this titanic senior battle in which the pot boiled over on two occasions.

Even though the rules ordain that the referee should have on each occasion ordered two men to the side-line, I have no doubt that he was indulgent, because the feuds were fought with fists rather than hurleys.

While Tipperary's margin was meagre enough, not even the most enthusiastic Cork follower could challenge the justice of the result. It might be argued that Cork could have won, but had they finished on top, the result would have been entirely at variance with the trend of the exchanges.

The real merit of the Premier County's triumph is illustrated by the fact that they came through, although out-classed for most of the hour in the vital midfield area.

There, Terry Kelly was so rampant that the Tipperary men decided to switch Theo English and Tom Ryan in the hope that the Cork player's activities would be curbed; but the losers' mentors, adopting the maxim, "anything you can do, we can do better," switched Kelly back on Ryan, who only came into the game and then spasmodically, when Cork for some reason that was a mystery to me moved Kelly to the "mark".

That Cork put in such a tremendous effort with what many considered a very much substandard side is a tribute to their hurling gallantry. There is a saying as old as hurling that "Cork are always a big danger in the Munster final," and never was the observation more truly borne out.

For most of the hour they tied down the Tipperary danger men, Jimmy Doyle and Liam Devaney, and that the home side won was in large measure due to a purple patch that Jimmy Doyle struck between the 6th and 14th minute of the second half.

During this period, he put on five points of his personal tally of a goal and eight points. In that spell, not even the most devoted attention of his rival, Denis O'Riordan, was of the slightest avail.

Set the Pattern

Devaney, too, played his part magnificently, and there is little doubt that he would have left an even greater imprint on the game had not Gerry O'Sullivan often enjoyed a latitude that must have exasperated Tipperary followers.

The tempo of the fray was set in the first minute when Paddy Barry had a glorious goal for Cork, in a game in which scores were level three times.

When the losers led by 2-4 to 2-2 after 21 minutes, many Tipperary hearts must have been a-flutter, and although the winners put on another goal and a point before the interval, their supporters must have been aghast when Cork scored four points in the first five minutes of the second half.

A daring goal by Sean McLoughlin somewhat soothed fevered Tipperary brows, and then it was that Jimmy Doyle stole the show, and the game from Cork, in a glorious spell which I have no doubt he will ever recall with a glow of satisfaction.

To me it seemed that Cork entered the fray incensed that they were generally regarded as outsiders and, in consequence, many of their side played well above themselves, none more so than Kelly and Duggan.

Cork played with a frenzy that was as effective as it was inspiring, but Tipperary, knocked out of the stride into which they had stormed in earlier matches, stood shoulder to shoulder with their rivals, and although the losers imposed their will to a large degree, their efforts were futile against men of inflexible will and great talents.

When Tipperary led by six points twelve minutes after the resumption it seemed that Cork had expended all they had to offer, but not a bit of it, and up to a couple of minutes from the end the result was in such doubt that those in the attendance with an affinity with either side must have experienced what might be termed tortuous delights.

When Tipperary folk look back on the match I feel sure that they will record the warmest votes of thanks to Jimmy Doyle, Devancy, Sean McLoughlin, Liam Connolly, Tony Wall, Mick Burns, Mick Maher, Tom Moloughney and Theo English in the second half.

The game was but a minute old when Barry put through the Tipperary defence for a gem of a goal. In the second minute Jimmy Doyle opened Tipperary's account with a point, a score which Kelly negatived in the 4th minute.

Devaney then put on a Tipperary point, and in quicker time than it takes to relate, Quane had a like score for Cork.

Near the end of the quarter, Moloughney had a Tipperary point, and half a minute later Liam Connolly tore the Cork defence to ribbons when he careered through for a wonderful goal.

Barry goaled for Cork after the whistle

had gone for an infringement, and from a later free Ring levelled. Seconds later Connolly made a goal for McLoughlin, but within two minutes Cork were again level, when Barry goaled from a Ring free, and in the 21st minute Cork shot ahead, when Ring had a capital point.

In the 27th minute Jimmy Doyle gave Mick Cashman no chance with a jet propelled shot, and just on the interval the same player pointed a free to leave the half-time tally **Tipperary, 3-4; Cork, 2-4.**

Within a minute of the re-start Joe Twomey shook off the attentions of Mick Burns to score a Cork point, and Ring followed with a point from a free and a like score from play, when it seemed that he had the goal at his mercy.

On the stroke of the 5th minute, Quane again put Cork in front with a point, but a minute later McLoughlin cheered Tipperary with a goal. Jimmy Doyle followed with four great points, one of them from a free, but the issue was wide open when Dowling crashed the ball to the Tipperary net in the 13th minute.

Jimmy Doyle quickly followed with a point from a free, and just at the end of the quarter Duggan had a similar score for Cork. Two minutes later, McLoughlin was unlucky when a shot by him brought only a point instead of a goal.

Ring tacked on a point from a free, but Donie Nealon and Jimmy Doyle (free) quickly followed with Tipperary points. Ring answered with a Cork point, but Wall stretched Tipperary's lead with a point from a free about 80 yards out. Almost on the close of time Quane worked through for Cork's last goal.

Tipperary: T. Moloney; M. Hassett, M. Maher, K. Carey; M. Burns, T. Wall (capt.), John Doyle; T. Ryan, T. English; Jimmy Doyle, L. Devaney, D. Nealon; L. Connolly, T. Moloughney, S. McLoughlin.
Cork: M. Cashman; J. Brohan, J. Lyons, S. French; M. McCarthy, J. O'Sullivan, D. O'Riordan; P. Duggan, T. Kelly; P. Barry, E. Goulding, J. Twomey (capt.); L. Dowling, M. Quane, C. Ring. **Subs:** D. Murphy for French, N. Gallagher for Twomey, J. Bennett for Duggan.
Referee: G. Fitzgerald (Limerick).

Waterford Triumph As Tipperary Waste Golden Chances

WATERFORD 0-11 : TIPPERARY 0-8

It is the scores that count. Rarely, if indeed ever, can that age-old hurling maxim have been more thoroughly vindicated than at Limerick Gaelic Grounds yesterday when Waterford defeated All-Ireland champions Tipperary by 0-11 to 0-8 in the Munster senior final, played in sweltering heat before an attendance of over 36,000.

There was much in this contest to sustain Tipperary lamentations that the match was thrown away. But in the final analysis superiority through the field, galling misses and incredible wides are an indictment rather than a defence of a team.

Tipperary, who once again failed in their bid to win four successive Munster titles, should have been as safe at the interval as the hay which was got off the ground in yesterday's brilliant sunshine.

In the first thirteen minutes they shot no fewer than eight wides and finished with a total of sixteen such "offences" to their discredit.

The real disparity between the sides in that opening half is not however, truly revealed until one puts it on record that Waterford did not force their second over until the eighteenth minute after the throw-in.

Waterford, it will also be argued, were able to get only three points from play in an hour's hurling but who is so inspired as to dogmatise as to what would have happened on more than a few of the occasions that the Tipperary defence had cause to throw discretion to the wind.

Waterford, even those who were festooned with blue and gold colours must admit, also missed chances, but although supplied by a half inch pipe line as against the spate of opportunities that Tipperary enjoyed but failed to utilise, they ran up 11 points as against eight. That is what counts. Missed chances do not.

The uncertainty as to the outcome from an early stage, due to the weak—one might almost say feeble—finish of the Tipperary attack, made it an absorbing struggle and the tenseness of the final minutes must have aroused even those with no attachment to either side.

There was a deal of mediocre striking and both sets of forwards seemed entirely innocent of the art of goal scoring.

Indeed when one turns to apportion shares of the victory bouquet to Waterford men, Austin Flynn, Ned Power and Tom Cunningham stand far ahead of their colleagues in the parade to the rostrum.

This assuredly was a Flynn better than ever in the past, and he has many valiant performances to his credit in the Decies jersey.

He played all through with a calculated assurance that saved his side time and again and he so often averted danger when all seemed lost that one could be forgiven for thinking that his hurley was as flexible as a switch. He used it to good effect even when it appeared he had no room to breathe.

In Tipperary they rate Sean McLoughlin the "terror of goal-keepers". He often has been, but he was rendered entirely harmless by a rampant Cunningham, who generously distributed his services in areas which, strictly speaking, were not his concern.

Power in goal brought off a few saves that would have done credit to Ollie Walsh and his pucking out of the ball in the second half was of such length that each initiated a Waterford attack.

Grimes's Part

Although he was outplayed by John Doyle in the open and close exchanges, Phil Grimes can also claim much credit for the victory because of seemingly radar controlled striking of frees. He was also ever-vigilant, so eager that he would not even take time in the second half to discard his jersey, the back of which had been torn away in one of the winners' fierce raids.

After that quartet, Waterford were much

of a muchness, efficiency rather than brilliance being the stamp of the eleven.

In flashes, however, Tom Cheasty, Mick Flannelly and Joe Condon, Frankie Walsh and Martin Og Morrissey caused supporters to applaud lustily their endeavour. Morrissey, however, was outplayed by Larry Kiely who, unfortunately from a Tipperary viewpoint, had to move from the "mark".

Even after knocks had caused him to be moved to full forward, the Glengoole man, who carried an injured shoulder into the fray, stood out head and shoulders over all his colleagues in the losers' forward division.

Other Tipperarymen who can wash their hands clean of the defeat are John Doyle, Mick Maher, Kieran Carey, Tony Wall, who had the better of the duel with Cheasty, Mick Burns, until forced to retire with an injury, Theo English and Donie Nealon.

Performed Well

In view of the fact that Tipperary lost, it may be regarded as irrational to accord so many special mention, but believe me they deserved to be distinguished from their team-mates. They performed their task splendidly. The others did not.

Following a fumble by Mounsey, who must have been possessed of the jitters, Waterford opened the scoring with a point by Condon in the third minute. In all truth, Tipperary were lucky that Grimes was fractionally late on the scene after the goalkeeper committed his error.

In the fourth minute, English levelled from a line-ball about 40 yards, but in the fifth minute Waterford regained the lead when Grimes pointed a free from about 50 yards out.

In the seventh minute Jimmy Doyle made a point by Nealon and four minutes later English did spade work for a point by Jimmy Doyle. Early in the second quarter, Jimmy Doyle put Tipperary ahead with a point from a free and in the 20th minute, Devaney had a capital point for the losers. Three minutes before the interval Grimes had a point from a placed ball to leave the half-time score **Tipperary, 0-5; Waterford, 0-3.**

Less than three minutes after the restart, Jimmy Doyle had a great point for the champions but then came two crushing blows to Tipperary. First a goal by Sean McLoughlin was disallowed after a great run by John McKenna. McLoughlin rammed the ball to the net but he was guilty of bad judgment in remaining in the "square" although he had all the time in the world to get outside it before making his stroke.

Then a minute later, McKenna sent wide when it appeared the only thing he could do was to put the ball in the net.

Those nails in the coffin of the Tipperary's hopes were not hammered, but sledged home, by five points between the 8th and 13th minutes by Grimes (free, 8th minute), Walsh (9 mins.), Grimes (free, 11 mins.), Power (12 mins.), and Grimes (free, 13 mins.).

A grand point by Jimmy Doyle in the 18th minute kept Tipperary in the hunt, and the flagging hopes of supporters of the champions were revived in the 19th minute when English laid on a point by Kiely.

Hit Back

Waterford now apparently in danger, tucked up their sleeves in earnest and hit back with three points by Grimes from frees in the 20th, 23rd and 26th minutes. Tipperary, however, were not done with, but as time was running out a very promising attack was ruined by Devaney who almost outdid McKenna when sending wide with a goal at his mercy.

Waterford: N. Power; T. Cunningham, A. Flynn, J. Byrne; L. Guinan, M. Og Morrissey, J. Irish, J. Meaney, J. Condon (capt.); M. Flannelly, T. Cheasty, F. Walsh; S. Power, J. Barron, P. Grimes. **Sub:** M. Dempsey (for Meaney).

Tipperary: R. Mounsey; John Doyle, M. Maher, K. Carey; M. Burns, T. Wall, P. Ryan; T. English, D. Nealon; Jimmy Doyle, L. Kiely, T. Ryan; J. McKenna, L. Devaney, S. McLoughlin (capt.). **Subs:** M. Murphy (for Burns), L. Connolly (for Ryan).

Referee: G. Fitzgerald (Limerick).

Limerick The Champions
—Pointed "70" Foils Tipp

LIMERICK 6-7 (25) : TIPPERARY 2-18 (24)

Game, match, contest, how insipid and almost meaningless do such words seem when one turns to relate the events as they torrented on each other in a fantastic finish to the Munster Senior Hurling Championship final in which Limerick, who had not won the title since 1955, defeated Tipperary by 6-7 to 2-18 on an ideal hurling day before an attendance of 41,723 at Semple Stadium, Thurles, yesterday.

Rarely if ever can there have been a more dramatic and tempestuous finish to a southern decider in which Limerick prevailed by virtue of a last gasp and controversial point from a "70" by Richie Bennis. So exciting and uplifting was the finish for neutrals, never mind those with affinity with either side, that it mattered not at all that the general quality of performance did not match the other ingredients which made it such a joyous spectacle.

From the 31st minute of the second half right to the call of time, memorable spectacles and happenings so cascaded on each other that the memory of some of them is even now misted by the epic last moments of the encounter.

With time running out, and the sides level at 6-6 to 2-18, a massed Limerick onslaught brought a "70". In the welter of excitement, there was a delay in the placing of the ball for the puck.

When the man in charge spoke to Bennis and pointed to his watch we knew, as I later confirmed with the Clarecastle official, that he told the player that he must score direct from the "70"—if anyone else touched the ball a score would not be valid and we would have another day.

But just as nonchalantly as in the National League final between the same counties in Cork two years ago, the Patrickswell player sent the last ball of the game truly between the posts.

The match which opened at a devastating pace really began to electrify the attendance in the 33rd minute of the second half. There were, to be sure, earlier glorious events and feats, but they were confined to the shadows or the fringes of the battle royal by the happenings in the last seven minutes.

Tipperary, 2-1 to 0-0 in arrears after 11 minutes, leaders by 2-9 to 3-2 at the interval, found themselves 6-3 to 2-11 behind 13 minutes after the restart. Going into the last quarter, the tally stood Limerick 6-4, Tipperary 2-13, but between the 24th and 33rd minutes the losers put on three points to level the scores.

A minute later Tipperary forged a point ahead but points in the 36th and 37th minutes regained the advantage for Limerick. A point by the home county 90 seconds from the end seemed to ensure that the game would end in stalemate, but Limerick, to their credit, came again in an avalanche and forced a "70", which brought the magnificent winner.

It will add greatly to the glamour and the recollections of the wonderful Limerick day that their success was achieved on "enemy" ground. While not even the most grudging Limerick man could carp had the victors been held to level scoring, I feel equally positive that justice was done in the outcome.

Throughout the 80 minutes, Limerick struck infinitely many better balls than did their rivals; and even though the losers had 20 scores to the winners' 13, there is no doubt in my mind that the visitors were the more even side through the field on a day on which both teams were lopsided.

Despite the failure of some Limerick celebrities to live up to their rating they were not in any sector of the field so ineffectively served as were Tipperary in the full back line, despite the splendid display turned in by right corner man Jim Fogarty.

Tipperary also committed grave tactical

errors in the last quarter—on a number of occasions they worked feverishly for goals when points which in the long run might have proved worth a bagful of goals were there for the taking.

Concession of six goals is its own indictment of the losers' defence, which also creaked ominously in the half line until Noel Dwyer moved back to the defence to take over from Jimmy Crampton.

It further impaired Tipperary's efficiency that long clearances out of the defence were the exception rather than the rule, and had it not been for centre-forward Mick Roche's astuteness in playing something of the role of a midfielder, the losers' attack would surely have hungered for opportunities.

A switch decided upon in the half-time huddle of the Limerick selectors had a profound influence in fashioning the triumph. The moment which brought Bernie Hartigan from left half forward to midfield wiped out an early Tipperary ascendancy in the sector, established mainly by the endeavours of Seamus Hogan, who continued to battle valiantly against the rampaging Limerickmen.

This Hartigan of the second half was the real Hartigan that Limerick hurling followers so esteem, and in my book he takes second place in the honours list because of the powerhouse of hurling he was after the change of ends.

Others in the winning side who will also be the toast of supporters in the days ahead are magnificent goalkeeper Seamus Horgan, John Foley, first at wing half back and in the second half in the centre of the line, Eamonn Grimes, Liam O'Donoghue, Frankie Nolan and converted full forward Ned Rea, who proved an insoluble problem for John Kelly, who had a match the memory of which he will not cherish.

Richie Bennis, of course, deserves to be singled out above all his colleagues, even over Hartigan. In addition to the astonishing aplomb with which he took the winning score, it was his points from immaculate frees that kept his side in the hunt in the supercharged closing stages.

Best for Tipperary were Fogarty, the losers' man of the match, Len Gaynor, Hogan, Francis Loughnane, Roche and Michael Keating, who showed flashes of his old genius and might with profit have been more generously supplied.

Some Tipperary folk were dogmatic that not only was Bennis's 70 shot wide of the post but that the award of the 70 was a wrong decision. I am not in a position to express an opinion about the legality or otherwise of the 70 award, but the winning ball seemed a true point from my vantage point in the stand.

One of the umpires, Michael Keane (Clarecastle) told me after the game that, following his signalling of the winning point, he "got a dig of a hurley from a Tipperary back"—a man about whose identity the official had no doubt whatever.

Scorers for Limerick were F. Nolan (2-1), E. Cregan (2-0), M. Dowling (1-0), R. Bennis (1-5, goal and 5 points from frees and a point from 70) and L. O'Donoghue (0-1). Tipperary replied per F. Loughnane (2-10), (7 points from frees), M. Keating (0-4), S. Hogan (0-2 from frees), N. O'Dwyer (0-1) and J. Flanagan (0-1).
Limerick: S. Horgan; W. Moore, P. Hartigan, J. O'Brien, P. Bennis, J. O'Donnell, J. Foley; R. Bennis, E. Grimes (Capt.); L. O'Donoghue, M. Dowling, B. Hartigan; F. Nolan, E. Rea, E. Cregan. **Sub.**—T. Ryan (for O'Donnell, at start of second half).
Tipperary: T. Murphy; J. Fogarty, J. Kelly, J. Gleeson; J. Crampton, T. O'Connor, L. Gaynor; S. Hogan, P.J. Ryan; F. Loughnane (Capt.), M. Roche, N. O'Dwyer; J. Flanagan, R. Ryan, M. Keating. **Subs.** J. Ryan (for Crampton, 56 mins.), D. Ryan (for J. Ryan, 75 mins.).
Referee: M. Slattery (Clare).

Tailpiece: An irritating feature of the game was the number of delays in replacing balls which were not returned when they went out among spectators in the embankments. The replacements had to be delivered from the midfield area in each instance. One would imagine that it would have been seen to that the umpires would be supplied with spare balls to meet such situations. At half time an astonishing announcement came over the public address system—an appeal for about half a dozen balls which were badly needed.

Richie Bennis' last-gasp point from a "70" gave the title to Limerick.

Eamonn Grimes

Eamonn Cregan scored two goals for Limerick in the 1973 final

47

Cork Keep Title

Backs See Champs Through Tense Tie

CORK 0-13 : CLARE 0-11

A superb defence that was cool, calm, collected and tight as the proverbial clam carried Cork to a fourth on the trot and 37th in all Munster S.H. Championship title at overcrowded—some thousands were left outside—overcast Semple Stadium, Thurles, yesterday. Yet, in the heel of the hunt, there could be no doubting the merit of the All-Ireland champions two-point win over the disappointing League title-holders.

Cork, severely handicapped through the twin loss of defender Brian Murphy and forward star Seanie O'Leary, looked to have blown it by the half-way stage when, with wind advantage they led only by 0-5 to 0-3. Worse still, their forwards had failed to score—their tally coming from four long-range John Horgan frees and a fine effort from midfielder Tom Cashman.

Yet, their defence had played heroically in that 35 minutes of untidy, tension-affected play but the only sign of Cork nerves was one fumbled catch by Martin Coleman. Clare, by comparison were full of running but while the defence had looked good and their forwards had scored they had failed to make any headway down the middle.

Unbelievably the Corkmen had run up a shoddy total of 13 wides but Ray Cummins and Charlie McCarthy apart there was little real menace in the forward set-up. The sector underwent changes after the interval and these alterations and likely a blistering pep-talk helped further to hustle Clare out of their normal game.

Yet, in this the first goal-less Munster hurling final since '63 and only the second such in all, Cork had to await the 46th minute for their first point from play. It fell to Ray Cummins who, securing deep on the right, steered it between the uprights from a remarkably acute angle.

That point put the All-Ireland champions five points ahead and while Clare, to their credit, came fighting back their headway was mainly through frees. Indeed, in the whole 70 minutes the winners managed only two points from play and only two of these were scored by a forward while the losers did slightly better by slotting one more via this route.

The lack of goals apart this Munster final will go down as the most forgettable for many years. Tension appeared to be the main bugbear while the power of the rival defenders and their commitment to the task in hand contrived to make it an off day for forwards.

It was therefore, a poor return for all but the Corkmen in the bumper attendance of 54,181 who paid over £70,000 for the privilege of watching this eighth in all Cork-Clare decider. On reflection, however, one is forced to the conclusion that while Clare were physically primed for the occasion, they were less than right mentally.

As I saw it the game was there for the taking, especially at the interval when, set to take wind advantage—Sean Stack, who won the toss, had conceded this to the winners—they were but a pair of points in arrears. Yet, within minutes, they were struggling at midfield and suddenly looking less confident in defence.

For this, much of the credit belongs to the re-charged Corkmen and more particularly to the younger members of that group. And the hero of heroes among the youngsters was Blackrock's Tom Cashman, son of a famous father and at 21 already in possession of a Carrolls All-Star award.

Young Tom, who like his dad, Mick, started in goal, gave a marvellous display of classy midfield play while little behind were clubmate, Dermot McCurtain, and Bishopstown's Johnny Crowley, who between them extracted much of the teeth from the Banner attack. Indeed, such was the effectiveness of

CORK, MUNSTER HURLING CHAMPIONS 1978

49

Seamus Durack, the Clare keeper

the defence as a whole that Martin Coleman had nothing to worry about in the second half.

Tim Crowley, who had an undistinguished first half at midfield, did much better when switched to right half-forward, but apart from Ray Cummins' fine fetching and the splendid accuracy of Charlie McCarthy from frees there was nothing exciting about the approach of this so feared attack. Truly Seanie O'Leary was missed from the area.

Clare had heroes in goalkeeper Seamus Durack and right half-back Ger Loughnane. Seamus, who had many superb saves to his credit, sallied upfield on two occasions in a desperate attempt to get the attack moving.

Ger, who in recent months had failed to sustain the high standard he has set himself came roaring back to his best. Yet, few faults could be found with defence, where Sean Hehir and Sean Stack alternated between wing and centre-back in attempting to counter the Cork moves.

Further afield the Bannermen had little to offer on this occasion and one must question the wisdom of Colm Honan in going for a point with his final free in the 68th minute. Only a goal would then have saved the challengers and who knows but that a low, blockbusting shot or a lobbed free might have paved the way to it.

Scorers: Cork, C. McCarthy (0-5), J. Morgan (0-4), R. Cummins (0-2), T. Cashman, T. Crowley (0-1 each). **Clare,** C. Honan (0-6), G. Loughnane, M. Moroney, J. Callinan, N. Casey, E. O'Connor (0-1 each).
Cork: M. Coleman; D. Burns, M. O'Doherty, J. Horgan; D. McCurtain, J. Crowley, D. Coughlan; T. Cashman, T. Crowley; G. McCarthy, J. Barry-Murphy, P. Moylan; C. McCarthy, R. Cummins, M. Malone. **Subs:** E . O'Donoghue (for Malone), P. Horgan (for Moylan).
Clare: S. Durack; J. O'Gorman, J. Power, J. McMahon; G. Loughnane, S. Hehir, S. Stack; M. Moroney, J. Callinan; J. McNamara, N. Casey, C. Honan; P. O'Connor, M. McKeogh, E. O'Connor. **Sub:** B. Gilligan (for McKeogh).
Referee: J. Moloney (Tipperary)

Limerick Show
True Courage

LIMERICK 2-14 : CORK 2-10

An All-Ireland series without the traditional giants Cork, Kilkenny, Tipperary and Wexford, seemed unthinkable at season's start, but gallant Limerick made it so at sunny, spectacular and cold Semple Stadium, Thurles, yesterday. This they did by pressurising the record chasing champion Corkmen from start to finish and by presenting a defensive screen that pushed back the frontiers of courage and commitment to ring up the county's 15th Munster S.H.C. success and first since '74 before an attendance of 43,090.

With the sun breaking the cloud barrier Semple Stadium provided a magnificent canvas for a game that was fast, tough and, by the finish, grippingly exciting. Yet, there were spells of undistinguished play and even gross mis-hitting as the Shannonsiders surging back from their league final defeat by this opposition, led almost from start to finish.

Indeed, the holders, a goal adrift as early as the fourth minute, succeeded only in drawing level and never once getting their noses in front. The Corkmen, who won the toss and conceded a fresh to strong wind advantage to their rivals, trailed by four points at the break—1-7 to 1-3—and got to within two before being pegged at that by a superbly defiant winner's rearguard.

Limerick had, of course, done their homework. Denied victory by this opposition in the May 4 League final and in the replay two weeks later, they had analysed that failure with a thoroughness that was all but Teutonic; the big question being would time permit the repairs to be made?

Carried Out

Essentially the repairs were carried out to the half forward line—the area from which Cork were permitted to dictate in the earlier meeting at Pairc Ui Chaoimh. Yet, the suggestion that the repairs were effected at the cost of weakening elsewhere, was given further ammunition when Liam O'Donoghue, switched from half back to the engine room area of attack, had to be pulled back after 26 minutes.

Yet, such was the brilliance of the sturdy Mungretmen that the Limerick weakness at half back was not only sealed off but, paid for any amount of attacks. Furthermore, while not emerging as a classy forward, the "transplanted" Paudie Fitzmaurice ensured that Cork's efforts were largely defensive in his new surroundings at half forward.

Vieing with Liam O'Donoghue for the role of Limerick's hero among heroes was pint-sized Ollie O'Connor, who, after a subdued opening quarter blossomed into the all-go attacking artist he can be. In so doing he displayed valour far beyond the call of duty and crowned it all by grabbing a great goal and a point.

The goal was a gem in timing and execution for Cork, who had fallen five points behind eleven minutes into the second half, got within a brace one minute later. This was when Jimmy Barry Murphy, who had moved from wing to centre forward set up Seanie O'Leary and the Youghal man picked his spot to hammer home an unstoppable shot.

Given that injection Cork, who were never allowed to move with normal fluency suddenly looked full of menace but it hardly helped that handicapped skipper Dermot McCurtain had then to leave because of injury. The Blackrock lad, twice injured in the first half, seemed badly shaken following the second knock and he never recovered the flamboyance of his earlier play.

Let it be emphasised, nonetheless, that for all its fire and fury this was an exemplary exhibition of all-out sporting endeavour. Happily, it remained so even when both sides strained every sinew in a grand stand finish for the great prize of a spot in the All-Ireland final in September.

Unfortunately, such super sportsmanship did not extend onto the terraces where, at the Killinan end, we had a colourful crowd but with a very bleak outlook. This misguided group threw missiles onto the goal mouth to show their displeasure and play was held up on one occasion while Cork's John Horgan appealed—successfully—to their better natures.

Even they were happy with O'Leary's goal, which put the champions seeking record 6th successive and 39th in all Munster crown, in a strong challenging position. Five tension packed minutes elapsed before the next score followed, and this, significantly, fell to Limerick.

The scorer was that county's bundle of joy, Ollie O'Connor who picked up from a Donie Murray free, jinked his way past a couple of Cork defenders and a despairingly thrown hurley to crash the ball to the net. From then on in it was up to the Limerick defence and this, notably Murray, Leonard Enright and David Punch were magnificent—defiant, fearless and inspiring.

The opening goals were, by contrast, the result of defensive lapses. Limerick struck first when Timmie Murphy dropped Jimmy Carroll's shot and in the resultant melee Eamonn Cregan got the vital touch to push the ball home. The winners' defence was caught napping eight minutes later when Pat Horgan pulled to the left to leave only Dominic Punch facing Seanie O'Leary, Jimmy Barry Murphy and Eamonn O'Donoghue, and when the Glen Rovers man crossed O'Donoghue headed the queue to give Tommy Quaid no chance.

Horgan had been very effective early on against Mossie Carroll, getting the vital touch to completely foil the Limerick man's normally expert handling of the high through ball. Moreover, with Tim Crowley and Barry Murphy switching wings from the start the entire Limerick half back line was under heavy pressure.

For all that, the winners marshalling from the sideline was sometimes inspired and never less than splendid.

Cork edged midfield early on with John Fenton augmenting his control from play with admirable accuracy from frees. The Midleton man also had a right go at a 22nd minute semi penalty, but the brilliant Leonard Enright, manning the goal with Tommy Quaid and Mossie Carroll, parried the shot and then got it clear.

The final minutes were full of fire and the best hurling of the game as Cork, their forward line much changed, tried desperately to get through for vital scores. Yet it was in Limerick breakaways that Leesiders fate was sealed as the dispairing Corkmen conceded vital frees. The wiley Cregan, cool as ice, slotted each and every one over the bar.

Scorers: Limerick, E. Cregan (1-6 points from frees), O. O'Connor (1-1), David Punch (0-1), S. Foley, L. O'Donoghue, W. Fitzmaurice, J. Carroll, J. McKenna (0-1). **Cork,** J. Fenton, (0-6, 4 from frees), E. O'Donoghue (1-1), S. O'Leary (1-0), T. Crowley, P. Horgan, D. Coughlan (0-1 each).

Limerick: T. Quaid; D. Murray, J. Enright, Dom Punch; P. Fitzmaurice, M. Carroll, S. Foley; J. Carroll, David Punch; L. O'Donoghue, J. Flanagan, W. Fitzmaurice; O. O'Connor, J. McKenna, E. Cregan.

Cork: T . Murphy; B . Murphy, M. O'Doherty, J. Horgan; D. Coughlan, J. Crowley, D. MacCurtain; J. Fenton, T. Cashman; T. Crowley, P. Horgan, J. Barry-Murphy; S. O'Leary, R. Cummins, E. O'Donoghue. **Subs:** P. Moylan (for MacCurtain), C. McCarthy (for Cummins).

Referee: J.J. Landers (Waterford).

LIMERICK, MUNSTER HURLING CHAMPIONS 1980

Cork Win 41st Title Before 50,000 Crowd

CORK 4-15 : TIPPERARY 3-14

Four points down with six minutes remaining, Cork came off the ropes to stage a remarkable recovery at Semple Stadium in Thurles yesterday. Capitalising on vital breaks, the Leesiders finally topped Tipp by four points to land a third successive and 41st in all Munster S.H.C. title.

Before a bumper attendance of 50,093, in dry overcast conditions, these age old rivals rolled back the years to make the Centenary southern showdown something that it used to be—one of the greatest events in gaeldom, a trial of strength, skill and application that makes one proud to be Irish.

Cork won, and just about deservedly so, because they kept their heads and continued to hurl when the spoils appeared to have escaped their grasp. It would have to be added, however, that Lady Luck played her part in fashioning this latest success.

Turning over 2-10 to 3-5 ahead, the Leesiders appeared to lose their rhythm as Tipp, blossoming from half back, took a firm hold on the proceedings. The extent of the grip can be seen from a glance at the statistics.

One Point

The most stark fact for the reigning champions was that though the breeze assisted, they registered but one point between the 41st and 65th minutes. In that time, the losers shot from 3-7 to 3-14 and were moving with a gallantry and grit that seemed to ensure victory.

They even appeared to have survived a crushing body blow, the full effects of which, however, were later to be felt. This was the loss of Bobby Ryan, the team captain with what appeared from the Press Box to be a twisted ankle.

Bobby, who had been switched from left half back to left corner back, in the 13th minute, was playing an inspiring captain's part in his new role. In effect, his retirement amounted to a double blow for the challengers.

Pulled Back

This was because Seamus Power, the most progressive of their attackers, had to be pulled back to assume the onerous task of policing Tomas Mulcahy. This, Boherlahan's Power continued to do in style.

That said, the switch undoubtedly affected the firepower of the home attack. Nor can it have helped when Tipp, who had led briefly early on, and had fought back to level for a second time, were awarded a penalty in the 55th minute.

Power had to make the long trek up field to take the shot and it cannot have helped his nerves that Waterford referee, John Moore—who did an excellent job on his championship debut—had to further delay the taking in order to regulate the line of friend and foe alike.

It may be, of course, that Power deliberately went for his point, and the lead, but again from the Press Box it looked as if his target was the top left hand corner of the net. As it happened, he' got too much lift and pointed.

With the lead again, there was no holding Tipperary who, from goal out, hurled with even greater venom and purpose. Noel O'Dwyer pointed a free, Philip Kennedy converted a "70" and when O'Dwyer added what then seemed an insurance point, Cork's goose appeared cooked to a cinder.

Yet, things were happening which were to have a dynamic impact in a dramatic finish. One was the switching of Dennis Mulcahy to full back, where he sealed off an obvious weakness to atone, in large part, for a most undistinguished first half.

Another was the sudden emergence of Pat Hartnett, another Midletonian, into the powerful midfielder he can be. And yet more were the calling in of Tony O'Sullivan and the resultant switch of Tomas Mulcahy to centre forward.

Cork Comeback

Skipper Fenton, also from Midleton, started Cork's comeback with a pointed free in the 65th minute. A further effort was turned back by Seamus Power before Hartnett picked up from Mulcahy and when his shot was blocked, Tony O'Sullivan rammed the rebound to the net.

That put the sides level for a third time and Semple Stadium was gripped by a tension so taut as to be almost explosive. Fenton was wide. Plucky Tipp stormed back and while Michael Doyle might have scored, he chose to run left and pass.

The intended recipient of the pass was inrushing and better placed Nicholas English but it was superbly cut off by Dennis Mulcahy whose long breeze-assisted clearance was bound for over the bar.

John Sheedy correctly and smartly pulled it down but before he could complete his clearance, Seanie O'Leary swept in to slam the sliothar to the net.

Tipp's Agony

That was in the 69th minute but Tipp's agony was not complete. Forced back, once more, they conceded a free at midfield and John Fenton steered it all the way to put the icing on the cake for his team and to dramatically shatter the home side's hopes.

Thus ended a game which for sheer effort, fluency of play, excitement, and dramatic content, outshone all Munster finals of recent years. The first half was richly competitive but hardly memorable whereas the second period was fast, furious and packed with drama and excitement.

Cork won the toss and elected to play against the breeze and into the Killinan end. Pat Fitzelle took his place on the Tipp team but because of his recent injury, was unable to maintain his normally high standard beyond the 29th minute.

Cork opened with a point in the fifth minute but within 60 seconds they were rocked back on their heels by a home goal. It followed a free from Ralph O'Callaghan and in the melee which followed, Seamus Power poked the ball over the line.

Tomás Mulcahy on the run

It was the tonic Tipp needed but they too were rocked by two typical goals by the always-dangerous Jimmy Barry Murphy. Yet, ominously for Cork, their back line was seen to be suspect and they were severely punished when, after a Noel O'Dwyer shot had been blocked down, Donie O'Connell, then at the top of the left, cracked the rebound home.

Then, just into injury time, the home team goaled again. This time the marking was slack and the back play far too adventurous as Dennis Mulcahy failed to cut off a through ball which Michael Doyle then

John Fenton

Jimmy Barry Murphy

tapped on to a completely unmarked Nicholas English.

The second half was truly riveting and while Tipp were ultimately edged out, there can be no doubt that they are on the road back. Indeed, with a little luck yesterday they would have made it all the way back—in Munster, at least.

The Cork defence certainly benefitted from the switch of Dennis Mulcahy to full back and while John Hodgins gave little away, best here were Dermot MacCurtain and to a lesser degree, John Crowley and Tom Cashman. John Fenton had a splendid first half while Pat Hartnett hit his true form only nearing the end.

Scorers: Cork, J. Fenton (0-7, 0-6 frees), J. Barry Murphy (0-2), S. O'Leary (1-1), T. O'Sullivan (1-0), K. Hennessy (0-3), P. Horgan (0-3), P. Hartnett (0--1). **Tipperary,** S. Power (1-6, 0-4 frees), D. O'Connell (1-2), N. English (1-0), P. Kennedy (0-2, 0-1 from "70"), N. O'Dwyer (0-2, 0-1 from free), L. Maher, P. Dooley (0-1 each).

Cork: G. Cunningham; D. Mulcahy, D. O'Grady, J. Hodgkin, T. Cashman, J. Crowley, D. MacCurtain; J. Fenton, P. Hartnett; P. Horgan, T. Crowley, K. Hennessy; T. Mulcahy, Barry Murphy, S. O'Leary. **Subs:** J. Blake (for O'Grady), T. O'Sullivan (for T. Crowley), D. Walsh (for Horgan).

Tipperary: J. Sheedy; J. Bergin, J. Keogh, D. Cahill; P. Fitzelle, McIntyre, B. Ryan; R. O'Callaghan, P. Kennedy, N. English; D. O'Connell, L. Maher; M. Doyle, S. Power, N. O'Dwyer. **Subs:** J. Doyle (for Cahill), B. Heffernan (for Fitzelle), P. Dooley (for Ryan).

Referee: J. Moore (Waterford).

Tipp's Do-Or-Die
Approach Crushes Holders Cork

TIPPERARY 4-22 : CORK 1-22 (after extra time)

The dark cloud which brought despair to Tipperary for 16 years has lifted. The brilliant sunshine which now shines through has brought great joy, an emotion the blue and gold followers had often thought they would never again experience.

It took 170 minutes of passion, sweat, blood, tears, dreams, excitement and some marvellous hurling to bring Richard Stakelum up the steps of the Fitzgerald Stadium stand as Tipperary's emissary to repossess the Munster S.H. trophy.

Celebrations of an unprecedented nature had begun even before Terence Murray blew the final whistle. Cork, the great champions, had finally been forced into submission after a memorable struggle.

After the quality of Thurles one week ago we could not dare expect to be so lucky again in Killarney. The hurling was not as brilliant, but for sheer drama and entertainment this game was just as unforgettable.

Incredibly, Tipperary never held the lead until four minutes into the second period of extra time. They had to win the hard way, coming from behind at all times. That they succeeded made the victory all the sweeter.

Titanic Proportions

This really was a battle of titanic proportions. Cork knew they had escaped from hell a week earlier. They wanted it to be different this time and set out in sprightlier fashion to make it so. Until the last quarter of normal time they appeared to have done enough.

Yet Tipperary showed the character of real champions. They came back from six points down to level the game. They snatched a late point to bring the game to extra time. After the opening 15 minutes of that section of the game they were still behind, by one point.

Then events took a very unexpected turn. If anyone in Tipperary felt that Michael Doyle owed them a debt from 1984 then they were well-reimbursed.

Introduced as a sub in extra-time when the muscles of another hero Paul Delaney could take no more, Doyle pounced twice to beat Ger Cunningham and end the terrible famine for a proud hurling county.

A Famous Triumph

Donie O'Connell finished the game with a flourish and Tipperary's fourth goal. It brought the Cork players to their knees and enthusiastic Tipperary supporters, young and old, onto the field to celebrate a famous triumph.

Nine points is a flattering margin and does not properly reflect the Cork contribution to this epic. They gave all they had, played some delightful hurling and went within seconds of winning a record sixth Munster title in a row.

At the end the legs and lungs of too many players could not keep operating. The loss of the Cashman brothers through injury; the restrictions placed on John Fenton's movements also because of injury and the extra years took their toll.

It had been a hard, bruising battle. Sometimes it unfortunately got out of hand. Referee Murray never had proper control and some of his decisions mystified players and spectators.

Happily we will remember the game for better things. The occasion itself brought an atmosphere of gaiety and abandonment to Killarney. The game gladdened the hearts of the more than 45,000 people who saw it.

Great Defenders

New names will now be etched on the heroes' roll of honour. Tipperary have a tradition for great defenders. They have a unit now as good as most of what went before.

The full back line of the '60s was fondly known as "Hell's Kitchen". New titles will

57

now surely be created for the current incumbents. The Nenagh-Kilruane combination of John Heffernan, Conor Donovan and Seamus Gibson were quite outstanding again yesterday.

All through they hurled with power and passion. They tackled fiercely, got their hurleys to the ball when it appeared the battle for possession was lost, and their long clearances put pressure on the Cork defence.

In front of them Stakelum, Paul Delaney and John Kennedy recovered from shaky beginnings to finish in real style. Behind them Ken Hogan proved he has no nerves with a cool, composed performance.

That defence had a battle royal with Teddy McCarthy and Tony O'Sullivan for the 100 minutes. Tomas Mulcahy opened with a promise of producing the quality we know he possesses, but faded as the game went on. Kevin Hennessy worked tirelessly, but his contribution was restricted.

Cork began with Tom Cashman at midfield and he helped them to dominate this sector for much of the game. Pat Fitzelle began slowly for Tipperary, while Colm Bonner only opened up in the second half when Cashman went off injured. John Fenton scored 13 points from frees and 65's.

Tipperary did have problems in attack. They missed many easy scoring chances early in the game that could have proved very costly. The fluency that was in their game in Thurles never re-surfaced.

Only O'Connell and Pat Fox were consistently causing trouble for the Cork defence, with Fox being one of their outstanding figures.

Aidan Ryan, Nicholas English and Bobby Ryan featured only sporadically. The introduction of Martin McGrath brought about an improvement. He scored three points and generally did extremely well.

Commanded Position

Once again Richard Brown commanded his position at full back for Cork with authority. He was helpless when the three winning goals went in, trying to keep an eye on two or more forwards.

Jim Cashman excelled at right half back, but was then forced to retire at the start of extra time with a leg problem.

Tipperary had tried a number of forma-

Tipperary star Nicholas English heads for goal

tions in attack, but struggled there for 50 minutes. Only a delightful goal from English kept them in the game in the first half, at the end of which they trailed by five points— 1-5 to 1-10.

They hurled much better for most of the second half. Bonner began to impress at midfield and the half-back line, especially Delaney, began to provide power from the rear.

Midway through the second half they thought they had finally made the breakthrough. Fox was put clear and his sizzling shot seemed destined for the net. It rebounded off the upright, though the Tipperary camp felt it had come back into play off the stanchion at the back of the net.

TIPPERARY, MUNSTER SENIOR HURLING CHAMPIONS 1987

**Tipperary management trio (from left): Theo English,
Donie Nealon and "Babs" Keating**

Cork too had a goal disallowed, when Teddy McCarthy's effort was cancelled as Tony O'Sullivan was deemed to be in the square.

Extra-Time Welcomed

Everyone was happy when English took the soft option of a point in the last minute. Extra time was welcomed, except for those with weak hearts.

The players were weary but fought on. One wonders were Cork wise in leaving Fenton on the field solely for free taking duties, when he was barely able to run because of injury.

Fox and O'Connell earned the lead for Tipperary and then Doyle pounced to push the ball away from Cunningham after Brown had blocked O'Connor's effort. Three minutes later Bonner found Doyle free again inside the defence and the Holy Cross man grabbed the opportunity.

That goal prompted the Tipperary management team to start the celebrations. Michael Keating, Donie Nealon and Theo English hugged each other and County Chairman Michael Lowry. O'Connell's goal put the gloss on it. A nightmare was over.

Scorers: Tipperary, P. Fox (0-11, 7 frees), M. Doyle (2-0), D. O'Connell, N. English (1-1 each), A. Ryan, M. McGrath (0-3 each), P. Delaney (0-2, both 65s), P. Fitzelle (0-1). **Cork,** J. Fenton (0-13, 10 frees, 3 65s), T. Mulcahy (1-2), T. McCarthy, T. O'Sullivan (0-3 each), G. Fitzgerald (0-1).

Tipperary: K. Hogan; J. Heffernan, C. Donovan, S. Gibson; R. Stakelum, J. Kennedy, P. Delaney; C. Bonner, P. Fitzelle, G. Williams; D. O'Connell, A. Ryan; P. Fox, N. English, B. Ryan. **Subs:** M. McGrath for Williams. In extra time: M. Doyle for Delaney; G. Stapleton for Donovan.

Cork: G. Cunningham; D. Mulcahy, R. Brown, J. Crowley; J. Cashman, P. Hartnett, D. Walsh; J. Fenton, T. Cashman; M. Mullins, T. McCarthy, T. O'Sullivan; K. Kingston, K. Hennessy, T. Mulcahy. **Subs:** G. Fitzgerald for Mullins, P. O'Connor for T. Cashman, J. Fitzgibbon for Kingston. In extra time: S. O'Gorman for J. Cashman, Mullins for Fitzgibbon, D. McCurtain for Crowley.

Referee: T. Murray (Limerick).

Flying Fox Saves Tipp

CORK 4-10 (22) : TIPPERARY 2-16 (22)

If the replay of this Munster final is half as exciting, as tense, as competitive and passionate as this drawn game we will be well and truly content. Veteran watchers of Munster hurling could not recollect a game as riveting in the history of the championship.

As a unit Cork were the better team for most of the game. Too many Tipperary players were off form yesterday and it was left to the likes of John Madden, Michael Cleary and John Leahy to keep them in this game.

Cork's full forward trio of Ger Fitzgerald, Kevin Hennessy and John Fitzgibbon had toyed with the Tipperary defence at times and between them scored 4-4 yesterday.

One of Cork's lesser known players who will become more famous in future is Cathal Casey and he was the outstanding hurler on view. He started at wingback, moved to midfield and was majestic in both positions.

Jim Cashman had another happy day against Tipperary. His role was made easier than usual by Declan Ryan's inability to make any impact on the game.

Ryan was not the only Tipperary player to be out of touch. Nicholas English shook his head in disbelief at the end. Absolutely nothing went right for the hurling artist and even what he thought was a legitimate equalising point a minute from the end was waved wide.

Tipperary struggled throughout at midfield, although one must express surprise at the decision to remove Joe Hayes from the game in the second half.

It was in the defence, though, that Tipperary struggled most. The fullback line were very weak under the high ball from where three of Cork's four goals came. Only when Michael Ryan was introduced for the injured Conor O'Donovan was there ever an air of confidence in this sector.

Another substitute, Aidan Ryan, played a huge role in Tipperary's survival. He provided mobility and pace in an attack which had been lethargic up to his introduction.

Big Cormac Bonner did create some problems for Cork fullback Richard Brown, but, with his team-mate out of sorts, Tipperary gained little advantage.

One telling statistic about the performance of the Tipperary attack is that they shot fifteen wides to Cork's seven, with eight of these coming when they had the wind in their favour.

Cork were much more economical. The dropping ball paid dividends after just seven and a half minutes when Hennessy beat Tipperary goalkeeper Ken Hogan to a Brendan O'Sullivan delivery for Cork's first goal.

Two minutes later Fitzgerald tore the defence apart before laying off to Fitzgibbon to finish their second goal.

Less than seven minutes later Tomas Mulcahy strolled through a ragged defence and found Fitzgerald in glorious isolation to score the third goal. This left the scoreline at 3-3 to 0-5.

John Leahy provided some inspiration for Tipperary. He started and finished the move which brought Tipperary's first goal after twenty minutes to give them some respite from the battering. Cork led by 3-5 to 1-7 at half-time.

If the first half was spectacular, the second was even more so. It was heart-stopping stuff for the full 35 minutes with both goalkeepers called into action as goalmouth incidents piled up.

Cork brought on Pat Buckley at midfield and he was to make a telling impression. He was involved in the move which set up John Fitzgibbon for Cork's delightfully taken fourth goal, which restored Cork's lead of seven points.

At this stage we all thought Tipperary's chance was gone. They had been well beaten around the park and there seemed no way back. But Pat Fox was not giving up and with minutes remaining he pounced to collect a long delivery from Michael Ryan and he beat Ger Cunningham for a vital score.

The unlikely suddenly seemed possible. Michael Cleary pointed two frees to level the game with just seven minutes remaining. English then rid himself of John Considine for a moment and had a clear shot at goal for what might have been the match-winning score, but his effort was smothered by Cunningham's huge frame.

Hennessy restored Cork's advantage with two minutes remaining as the excitement threatened to generate thousands of cardiac arrests. English got another chance for glory when he kicked what he thought was a point.

So too did everybody else in the stadium except the umpire, who waved it wide despite the frank protests of English and Fox.

But referee Terence Murray allowed sufficient time for Fox to calmly score the equaliser just before full-time and set up a replay.

Cork: G. Cunningham; J. Considine, R. Brown, S. O'Gorman; S. McCarthy, J. Cashman, C. Casey; B. O'Sullivan, P. Hartnett; T. Mulcahy, M. Foley, T. O'Sullivan; G. Fitzgerald, K. Hennessy, J. Fitzgibbon. **Subs:** D. Quirke for Hartnett; P. Buckley for B. O'Sullivan; T. McCarthy for Quirke.

Tipperary: K. Hogan; P. Delaney, C. O'Donovan, N. Sheehy; J. Madden, B. Ryan, Conal Bonner; D. Carr, J. Hayes; M. Cleary, D. Ryan, J. Leahy; P. Fox, Cormac Bonner, N. English. **Subs:** M. Ryan for O'Donovan; A. Ryan for Hayes.

1991

Tipperary Come Back From The Dead

Replay

TIPPERARY 4-19 (31) : CORK 4-15 (27)

Semple Stadium in Thurles has been the location for many an epic battle, and yesterday's Munster final replay ranks with the best of them. Even the nerve ends of the neutral were taut, the pulses racing as Tipperary snatched back the Munster title Cork relieved them of last year.

It was a game which will be remembered for many great things—the intensity of the battle, the fire and brimstone in the wearying heat and the great skill.

Unfortunately, poor crowd control led to numerous pitch invasions by spectators, forcing referee Terence Murray to play six minutes overtime.

It will also be remembered for the battering of Ger Cunningham's goal in the second-half by spectators on the Killinan end who should be ashamed.

Happily, our memories will also consist of one of the great comebacks in the history of the ancient game.

When Kevin Hennessy scored a brilliant goal after 49 minutes to give Cork a nine point lead, it seemed the crown lay snugly on Cork's head.

Tipperary were not playing well and even their most ardent supporters were resigned to defeat.

In every battle a side needs a number of individuals full of bravery. Tipperary were without Nicholas English yesterday (he was replaced by Donie O'Connell) and had to look elsewhere. John Leahy took on that role, and grew as a man and as a hurler. Switched to midfield, he launched a rearguard action which proved spectacularly successful.

Of course he could not do it all on his

own. That is where Pat Fox came in. The knee might be gammy but the spirit is alive and he enjoyed one of his finest games in a long career.

Relative youngsters like Aidan Ryan, Michael Cleary and the young at heart Cormac Bonner, produced their moments of magic to give us a fascinating end to an extraordinary game.

For very long periods Cork looked very comfortable as champions. Sean O'Gorman recovered from a heavy knock in the first minute to give a powerful display.

Cathal Casey, Jim Cashman and Pat Hartnett drew a security cordon over the Cork 50 metre line and seemed to be leading the side to glory.

The gamble of re-introducing Teddy McCarthy was also working. He floated around the field in great style and when he was partnered by Pat Buckley they seemed indominatable.

Once again the Tipperary defence was in trouble. John Fitzgibbon goaled after 18 minutes, Ger Fitzgerald added another after 26 and both had acres of Semple's soil to reap.

Cork led by 2-8 to 1-7 at the break.

Aidan Ryan's introduction did not bring immediate relief. Tony O'Sullivan contributed his own stamp of class with three points in succession, to increase Cork's lead, and despite Cleary's three in reply, one would not have bet Lotto money on Tipperary's chances.

Then John Fitzgibbon made the space, layed off to Hennessy who seemed to have been crowded out of hope. He switched to his left and sent a screamer past Ken Hogan. 3-13 to 1-10, it was Cork's crown, we thought.

What it did was give life to Tipperary. Joe Hayes was now in the battle at midfield alongside Leahy and they combined to change the game.

Now Fox, Bonner and Aidan Ryan were getting the ball they wanted and which English would have relished if he were fit.

Bonner did much of the damage, racing out to meet the deliveries and opening up play for his corner and wing men.

Fox loved it, and capped a great display with a beautifully flicked goal when Ger Cunningham seemed to have a loose ball covered. Three points had preceded that so now the margin was just three points.

Battling

By now Cork looked like the victims: the flow was gone from their game. They met an explosion of newfound confidence and the lungs and legs could not respond.

Declan Carr's flicked goal from a Leahy delivery said it all.

They were level now and Aidan Ryan quickly gave Tipperary the lead. Although Pat Buckley equalised again for Cork, one sensed that Tipperary's momentum would bring them through.

Bonner and Fox gave them the lead and, as the game went into overtime, Aidan Ryan pounced spectacularly. Cork full back Richard Browne was in the process of clearing his lines when Ryan made a great block, ran on to the ball and rattled the net with a vital goal.

But the action was not yet over. Referee Murray was playing lost time when he awarded Cork a 20 metre free. Fitzgibbon stood over it and sent the ball to the net. Anything could have happened. But Tipperary would not be denied and Cleary polished off an astonishing day with two points to give Tipperary a most unlikely four-point victory.

Tipperary: K. Hogan, P. Delaney, N. Sheehy, M. Ryan, J. Madden, B. Ryan, Conal Bonner, D. Carr, Colm Bonner, D. Ryan, D. O'Connell, J. Leahy, P. Fox, Cormac Bonner, M. Cleary. **Subs:** A. Ryan for O'Connell, J. Hayes for Madden.

Cork: G. Cunningham, S. O'Gorman, R. Brown, D. Walsh, C. Casey, J. Cashman, P. Hartnett, B. O'Sullivan, T. McCarthy, T. Mulcahy, M. Foley, T. O'Sullivan, G. Fitzgerald, K. Hennessy, J. Fitzgibbon. **Subs:** P. Buckey for B. O'Sullivan.

Referee: T. Murray (Limerick).

The Roll of Honour
Munster Senior Hurling Finals

1887	Tipperary
1888	Tipperary/Clare *(Unfinished due to American 'invasion')*
1889	Clare
1890	Cork 2-0; Kerry 0-1
1891	Kerry 2-4; Limerick 0-1
1892	Cork 5-3; Kerry 2-5
1893	Cork 4-8; Limerick 0-0
1894	Cork 3-4; Tipperary 1-2
1895	Tipperary 7-8; Limerick 0-5
1896	Tipperary 7-9; Cork 2-3
1897	Limerick 4-9; Cork 1-6
1898	Tipperary 1-13; Cork 1-2
1899	Tipperary 5-16; Clare 0-8
1900	Tipperary 6-11; Kerry 1-9
1901	Cork 3-10; Clare 2-6
1902	Cork 2-9; Limerick 2-5
1903	Cork 5-16; Waterford 1-1
1904	Cork 7-12; Limerick 1-4
1905	Cork 7-12; Limerick 3-4
1906	Tipperary 3-4; Cork 0-9
1907	Cork 1-6; Tipperary 1-4
1908	Tipperary w.o.; Kerry scr.
1909	Tipperary 2-10; Cork 2-6
1910	Limerick 5-1; Tipperary 4-3
1911	Limerick 5-3; Tipperary 4-3
1912	Cork 5-1; Tipperary 3-1
1913	Tipperary 8-1; Cork 5-3
1914	Clare 3-2; Cork 3-1
1915	Cork 8-2; Clare 2-1
1916	Tipperary 5-0; Cork 1-1
1917	Tipperary 6-4; Limerick 3-1
1918	Limerick 11-3; Clare 1-2
1919	Cork 3-5; Limerick 1-6
1920	Cork 3-4; Limerick 0-5
1921	Limerick 5-2; Cork 1-2
1922	Tipperary 4-2; Limerick 1-4
1923	Limerick 2-3; Tipperary 1-0
1924	Tipperary 3-1; Limerick 2-2
1925	Tipperary 6-6; Waterford
1926	Cork 3-6; Tipperary 2-4
1927	Cork 5-3; Clare 3-4
1928	Cork 6-4; Clare 2-2
1929	Cork 4-4; Waterford 2-2
1930	Tipperary 6-4; Clare 2-8
1931	Cork 5-4; Waterford 1-2
1932	Clare 5-2; Cork 4-1
1933	Limerick 3-7; Waterford 1-2
1934	Limerick 4-8; Waterford 2-5
1935	Limerick 5-5; Tipperary 1-4
1936	Limerick 8-5; Tipperary 4-6
1937	Tipperary 6-3; Limerick 4-3
1938	Waterford 3-5; Clare 2-5
1939	Cork 4-3; Limerick 3-4
1940	Limerick 3-3; Cork 2-4
1941	Tipperary 5-4; Cork 2-5
1942	Cork 4-16; Tipperary 4-1
1943	Cork 2-13; Waterford 3-8
1944	Cork 4-6; Limerick 3-6
1945	Tipperary 4-3; Limerick 2-6
1946	Cork 3-8; Limerick 1-3
1947	Cork 2-6; Limerick 2-3
1948	Waterford 4-7; Cork 3-9
1949	Tipperary 1-16; Limerick 2-10
1950	Tipperary 2-17; Cork 3-11
1951	Tipperary 2-11; Cork 2-9
1952	Cork 1-11; Tipperary 2-6
1953	Cork 3-10; Tipperary 1-11
1954	Cork 2-8; Tipperary 1-8
1955	Limerick 2-16; Clare 2-6
1956	Cork 5-5; Limerick 3-5
1957	Waterford 1-11; Cork 1-6
1958	Tipperary 4-12; Waterford 1-5
1959	Waterford 3-9; Cork 2-9
1960	Tipperary 4-13; Cork 4-11
1961	Tipperary 3-6; Cork 0-7
1962	Tipperary 5-14; Waterford 2-3
1963	Waterford 0-11; Tipperary 0-8
1964	Tipperary 3-13; Cork 1-5
1965	Tipperary 4-11; Cork 0-5
1966	Cork 4-9; Waterford 2-9
1967	Tipperary 4-12; Clare 2-6
1968	Tipperary 2-13; Cork 1-7
1969	Cork 4-6; Tipperary 0-9
1970	Cork 3-10; Tipperary 3-8
1971	Tipperary 4-16; Limerick 3-18
1972	Cork 6-18; Clare 2-8
1973	Limerick 6-7; Tipperary 2-18
1974	Limerick 6-14; Clare 3-9
1975	Cork 3-14; Limerick 0-12
1976	Cork 3-15; Limerick 4-5
1977	Cork 4-15; Clare 4-10
1978	Cork 0-13; Clare 0-11
1979	Cork 2-14; Limerick 0-9
1980	Limerick 2-14; Cork 2-10
1981	Limerick 3-12; Clare 2-9
1982	Cork 5-31; Waterford 3-6
1983	Cork 3-22; Waterford 0-12
1984	Cork 4-15; Tipperary 3-14
1985	Cork 4-17; Tipperary 4-11
1986	Cork 2-18; Clare 3-12
1987	Tipperary 4-22; Cork 1-22
1988	Tipperary 2-19; Cork 1-13
1989	Tipperary 0-26; Waterford 2-8
1990	Cork 4-16; Tipperary 2-14
1991	Tipperary 4-19; Cork 4-15
1992	Cork 1-22; Limerick 3-11